C I R A K

GOD is a
Conservative
How Divine Order Restores Itself

Editor: Michael Cirak
Website: cirak.com

Copyright © 2025 Cirak
1st Edition
ISBN: 979-8-9941517-0-9

CONTENTS

CIRAK

GOD is a
Conservative

How Divine Order Restores Itself

PROLOGUE

This book is not about politics. It is not about left versus right, national debates, or party platforms. It is about something far deeper: being aligned versus misaligned, conscious versus conditioned, real versus inherited. It is about those who perceive life as it is, and those who see only what their conditioning allows them to see.

Humanity is passing through a profound crisis of perception. A vast machinery of distraction and narrative management has created the illusion of separateness—splitting populations into opposing camps and convincing each side that conflict is necessary for survival. Division is not merely a political strategy. It is a spiritual one. And it has reached a critical threshold.

The outcome of this moment will determine whether we return to alignment or descend further into the confusion that has already fractured so much of the human world. The stakes are incredibly high, even when they remain invisible to many. Under such conditions, neutrality becomes complicity. Every choice you make aligns you either with fear and provocation or with a deeper intelligence.

Those who see clearly already understand this. They recognize life's inherent design: how every imbalance pushes toward restoration, how every denial sharpens the truth, how every challenge expands your capacity to remain present in turbulence.

To speak of God as conservative is to speak of life as self-correcting—preserving what is real and dissolving what cannot endure. This book traces the current global forgetting while providing a blueprint for navigating those yet to come.

If you feel alienated by a world shouting about progress while it collapses into disorder, this book is for you. It offers a glimpse of the life that emerges when conditioned beliefs fall away—a life without anger, judgment, or fear. A life no longer trapped in right-versus-wrong thinking, but rooted in the immediacy of what is real.

This shift is not an event. It is the gradual peeling back of the mental constructs that once shaped your perception of reality. The veil falls not all at once, but piece by piece, until you begin to see the world as it actually is.

The purpose of this book is not to replace one belief system with another. It is to help you see the programming you've absorbed—and the consequences it has had on your health, relationships, decisions, and sense of meaning. Its aim is to free you from the mental architecture of an imposed reality so you can participate in life according to its design, not your conditioning. You should not accept any words contained herein that do not resonate. But you should be open-minded enough to explore whether they do.

A note on language: I use the word *God* throughout this book, but you may substitute any term that points to a higher intelligence—Source, Consciousness, Presence, Love, the Universe. Language is simply a pointer. What it points to is universal.

This is not a casual read. It is not for those seeking reassurance or comfort. It is for those willing to examine their worldview, question inherited beliefs, and encounter the deeper design of life.

Let's begin.

Part I

The Divine Architecture

CHAPTER I

GOD CONSCIOUSNESS

———◆———

God Consciousness is the awareness of a higher power behind everything that exists. In its truest form, it derives not from blind belief, but from an actual, physical response in your body. When something resonates, you experience it not as thought, but as *felt* truth.

With God Consciousness, you are open, present, clear, inheriting insights and perspectives that don't come from the mind. Instead, you receive guidance from within about which actions to take and what's right for you, even when rationally you may not understand why. Call it intuition, conscience, or inner knowing—it's God speaking through your body.

Most people, however, cannot hear this inner voice. Instead of responding to the reality of a situation, they react to their mental projection about it.

This mental conditioning hits us from all sides. From early childhood, we are conditioned to live in our heads, living out our beliefs, acting out our subconscious imprints. We mistake constant thinking for wisdom. We don't just *have* thoughts—we think we *are* our thoughts. And because everyone operates the same way, nobody questions it. The whole world is in the grip of the mind, and almost no one realizes it.

Ironically, it doesn't take much to notice just how unsettled and unreliable the mind is. If you try to keep your attention on your heartbeat, your breath, or even just a spot on the wall, you will quickly find that—within seconds—your attention starts to drift to random, unrelated things. Western psychology calls this *rumination*. The fickleness of the mind also reveals itself when you get together with family or friends to share old memories and realize that everyone remembers things differently. Or when you go shopping, how utterly frustrating it is to make up your mind. You wind up choosing *something* or *nothing* because the process of choosing has exhausted you.

The torment of the mind doesn't stop there. The mere thought of not knowing what tomorrow brings triggers anxiety in many, conjuring up fears of the worst-case scenario. Or you keep talking yourself out of pursuing your dreams because conditions are not yet ideal. Or you stay in a bad relationship for fear of starting over.

The mind finds problems in everything.
You can even fear success.

A busy mind prevents you from thinking clearly, sleeping peacefully, being present with loved ones, and enjoying your favorite activities. It keeps you distracted and disconnected from your body, from processing your emotions and becoming more self-aware. All the while, you're prone to making unwise decisions that keep you further misaligned. It shrinks your sense of possibilities, generates constant stress from indecision, and makes you obsess over how best to control the unknown—which is the future, which is life. With so much noise in your head, it's no wonder you become lost to your inner truth, cut off from God Consciousness.

But the vast majority of humans live exactly this way. They walk through life unaware how much their mind is distorting their lives—the consequences of which can be devastating. If left unchecked, the mind can justify or explain away any decision or course of action, no matter how illogical or inhumane. Its operating system relies on constantly judging, seeking validation, lingering on what has already happened, and amplifying what it wants to have happen. These tendencies of the mind—when given carte blanche—result in chronic stress, poor decision-making, meaninglessness, disillusionment, and mental illness. The widespread prevalence of these conditions is evidence of just how dominant the mind-identified state has become.

In contrast, those who live with God Consciousness are measurably happier, more stable, and enjoy a sense of peace, purpose, trust, and emotional well-being. This foundation enables them to stay focused, be still, live from inner guidance, and manifest their best lives. They walk through life fearlessly, embrace the mystery, and experience unity with the unfolding. Freed from the need to control, they are open to receiving, gracious in giving, and able to go with the flow whenever a pivot is required. God Consciousness is an open-minded, curious state where listening to your heart, following your blueprint, and honoring the gift of life are at the forefront.

With such an obvious contrast between mind identification and God Consciousness, it should be obvious which path benefits you more. But when you're in your head, you don't see the obviousness of it. You're not interested in personal growth and expanding your worldview. Instead, you look to maintain what you have and defend what you already believe in. You confuse quantity with clarity. You keep making plans and chasing goals in the belief that happiness is something you must generate for yourself.

All of this is rooted in a deep scarcity mindset, where you must constantly attain in order to survive. This state is one of ongoing anxiety, loneliness, and acrimony—living like the world is out to get you. It's no wonder, then, that forgiveness, compassion, and service are tall orders. There is not enough emotional space for you to connect with the common humanity of others. Or to recognize the love of creation that's in every being. Or to feel the peace, clarity, and stillness that resides within. When you take action from the calm, connected place of your conscience, your life looks very different.

The good news is, course correction is just a stone's throw away. In fact, life is constantly nudging you in that direction. To connect with God Consciousness, all you need to do is get out of your head and into your body, where resonance lives. Prayer, meditation, and even simple exercise can help you enter that state. Also, using your senses to connect with the natural world evokes presence. The call to reconnect is right there in front of you, so close, all the time.

But there is one major challenge that gets in the way. Over the course of your upbringing, your identity has become intertwined with your thoughts about yourself and the world. The result isn't just thinking—it's *compulsive thinking*, a constant stream of random thoughts that absorb all of your attention most of your time. No matter how aware you are of this, you can't seem to stop it—it's deeply entrenched in your nervous system. Clinical psychology studies show we spend at least half of our day lost in thought about things that are irrelevant to the task at hand. From a spiritual perspective—considering my experience working with people in higher education, retreat settings, and private study—that percentage is much, much higher. Overthinking affects nearly everyone.

If you reflect on your own life, you can probably tell you're almost never *not* thinking. And it's mostly about things you have no control over: things from the past that cannot be changed, and things about your future that cannot be predicted. We've been taught to plan out our life instead of living it. To script our path ahead of walking it. To get better at projecting—and if things happen differently, we beat ourselves up about it. To live in our heads, is to be in constant negotiation. It's no wonder we cannot feel our inner truth.

When you're lost in thought, visceral God Consciousness is absent.

If you're serious about coming out of suffering, a committed practice of cultivating self-awareness is required. The only thing that releases you from your thoughts is to become more aware of them. This is how you transcend your attachment to stories, to your *self,* to all the unconscious beliefs that steer your choices, limit your quality of life, and keep you stuck in the "little human."

With God Consciousness, all of that dissolves. You're no longer just *you*. You see yourself in everything, because you can feel that everything is infused by the same Source. It's in every flower, every bird, and every breath you take. On land, sea, and air, there isn't a molecule that isn't permeated by it.

Divine intelligence also regulates our bodies without us having to do a thing. Our heart knows how to beat, our organs know how to function, and our lungs know how to breathe air day and night. We receive endless inputs from our environment, and our bodies convert them into chemical processes, which in turn follow their inherent instructions. Our brain is the greatest receiver of all, organizing vague, formless energy patterns into coherent concepts and ideas. Trillions of cells in our bodies act in unison to make all of this happen. You don't have to navigate life without the intelligence that's already guiding everything.

It's important to note that there is nothing inherently *wrong* with the mind. It's an amazing tool as long as we use *it*, not the other way around. It's always on the lookout to keep us safe, and that is a good thing. It's only when we rely exclusively on our mental faculties to navigate life that we get caught up in projections about everything that can go wrong, and we lose touch with the deeper wisdom of where the real directives come from. We forget the quiet intelligence that turns an acorn into an oak. We forget that we're all made of the same stardust and return to the same origin.

As you grow more aware of yourself and your environment, you start seeing things *as they are*. It's hard work, but God's work is worth seeing. It's what every serious meditator, bible reader, and Zen master aspires to. But you've got to do the work. Awareness reveals itself in proportion to your sincerity.

With God Consciousness, you are the container through which life flows. You are the vessel through which the formless takes shape. You are fearless in all circumstances because you're essence is far bigger than your circumstances. You see every situation as an opportunity—not to exploit—but to co-create. You no longer live from lack because you already feel complete. You begin to taste the highest form of existence: letting yourself be. No judgments. No need to fix. Just pure acceptance. It's paradoxical to the mind, but acceptance moves you forward. It gets you unstuck, freeing you up to establish your connection to the divine.

When you make decisions from your inner knowing, you are no longer driven by the little human. You are now living in service to God's plan.

CHAPTER 2

MEANING

———◦———

Life is designed to challenge us and make us grow. Clinging to the familiar is one of the ways we suffer.

Growth is rarely comfortable—but stagnation, depression, and misery from feeling stuck is far more painful. If you want to experience flow and have a fulfilling life, it's essential to embrace growth.

For those willing to dig deeper, it raises the question: What are we growing towards? A better salary, a partner, an accomplishment? These are all nice ideas, but they are outcomes. Living for outcomes is not living. Outcomes happen *while* living.

Life's meaning is not found in stories, memories, or things we achieve or own. Meaning is not a thing we can create and hold onto. But rather, it's an ongoing state of connectedness to what is happening right now, and letting our awareness of the situation guide how we respond to it.

How can you tell how aligned you are? It's easy. Life mirrors your honesty with yourself instantly. When you're aligned, you feel good. When you're misaligned, you feel bad. Life is a precise and instant feedback mechanism. At any given point, it always reflects how honest you are with yourself. How honestly you listen to your conscience. How honestly you follow truth. It is from this place of honesty that your life becomes meaningful.

Meaning is not found in outcomes. It is found in the *happening* itself. It comes from being present as life unfolds. By responding to what's actually there, not dragging in baggage from the past. By no longer pretending you know what a situation should be. Meaning is found in the gap between the unknown becoming known, the formless becoming form, and the intangible becoming felt. Once you experience that place, control no longer feels necessary.

When you live in the mind-identified state, life feel disconnected, anxious, and small. Your entire life experience consists of the mind looking for every little threat, devising strategies of how to avoid what *could* happen, and insisting on what it thinks *should* happen. It becomes a life consumed by fear, lack, and random impulse—completely starved of mystery and aliveness, devoid of a sustainable foundation from which to engage with the physical dimension.

The reason you can't predict the future is precisely the reason why you wouldn't want to: life is like a geyser bursting with endless creativity. You can never hold onto anything long enough before something new appears. So much so that *nothing* ever happens as expected. Every new moment is entirely, utterly, irrevocably *new*. No two moments in your life are ever remotely alike.

All insights and inspiration flow from our relationship with the unknown. While the mind may fear it, our job is to stay connected to it, to allow the feeling of uncertainty. That is life, and it cannot and should not be predicted. It should be lived. It should be felt. It should be experienced in all the infinite ways you could never imagine.

**Even your imagination is limited to who
you currently are.**

To truly grow beyond yourself and expand into your fullest potential, you need to learn to show up and respond to what's there. While it may be human to have some preconceptions and expectations, they should be held very, very lightly.

The fullest experience of life is directly proportional to your readiness to let everything you know go. Over and over again. To see not what you want to see, but to see things as they are. To not judge right or wrong, but to allow what is. To question even the most well-trodden paths. The current moment is the only thing that's real and the most potent place to be. It's where life happens.

Life responds when you show up for what is actually here. When you say 'yes' to the co-creative dance. It's from this movement that you download divine wisdom and from which your *inner calling* arises.

Unfortunately, few modern societies embrace the notion of a divine blueprint. Instead, the path that is offered consists of job openings and lifestyle patterns designed to support the policies and economics of the most powerful interests and institutions, whose sole aim is to turn you into a lifetime consumer of their propaganda products.

The entire system has been designed to that end. From childhood, you're ushered into a life designed by others—into an ever-increasing pressure cooker of milestones you must achieve and timelines you must meet in order to reap the next reward and be seen as a successful contributor to society. This is how status and public image grow in importance.

The illusion is so tightly structured that you shouldn't feel bad for not seeing it. You're rushed from one station to the next with barely an opportunity to reflect on what you're doing and if it's really the way you want to live your life. Only at the tail end of your life, are you relatively free to do what you want. What could be more demoralizing than going most of the way feeling like your true life hasn't yet begun?

Moreover, the evidence is in plain sight. Just look around, and you can see that the day of supposed freedom and happiness never comes. There is no finish line where everything stands still and the pieces of your happiness fall into place. The reality of your plans always turns out different. Perhaps an economic crisis causes your nest egg to evaporate. Perhaps you struggle with depression from being an empty-nester. Perhaps you find yourself called to help an aging parent. Perhaps you give birth to a special needs child. Perhaps you never meet your special person and learn to be content on your own. Perhaps you meet them much later in life, and in the meantime, your discover talents you didn't know you had. And maybe, just maybe, you experience a spiritual awakening, and every plan you ever had for your life goes out the window because you realize everything you thought was real isn't.

**Chasing happiness guarantees you'll
never arrive.**

There is no better way to live your life than to let it unfold and take an active role in the unfolding. Meaning is found when you stop trying to create it and invite it in. But this requires making peace with the unknown—not fearing it as the mind does, but welcoming it as the most faithful ally you will ever have.

CHAPTER 3

TRUTH

No matter what circumstances a human being is born into, long before they learn anything about the world, they inherit an ancient imprint: the pull toward truth. It is not taught. It cannot be acquired. It is not the result of reasoning or even reflection. It is deeper than instinct. Every person carries this memory of truth—not as belief—but as the natural orientation of awareness.

And yet, the moment you arrive in the world, something strange happens. You start absorbing the beliefs of others—family patterns, cultural expectations, inherited fears, unexamined assumptions, generational wounds—and take them on as your own. You think with inherited thoughts and navigate life through a worldview you never chose.

By adolescence, you become fluent in pleasing others around you. You know which ideas are rewarded, which emotions are acceptable, which behavior garners you love. But this adaptability has nothing to do with who you really are. It's purely survival.

**A child learns to blend with the world
long before learning to see it.**

The split between *subjective truth* and *objective truth* begins here. Subjective truth—truth constructed by the mind—is inherently unstable. It depends on agreement and approval, and resists anything that challenges its story. One of the trademarks of subjective truth is that it constantly reinforces *otherness* and *separateness*. It keeps you at a distance, in a place of disconnect from yourself and others.

Objective truth, on the other hand, is truth derived from God Consciousness. It is universal in nature and requires... nothing. It does not rely on belief, argumentation, or consensus. It arises on its own from being present with the situation. It reveals itself when the mind stops filtering reality through its stories. Objective truth is always quiet because it doesn't need to insist on anything. You know it when you encounter it, because the body settles and your breath evens out. It's an unmistakable resonance that the body recognizes instantly. Subjective truth requires effort. Objective truth needs none.

Nothing challenges the mind more than objective truth because it dissolves the mind's complex illusion of authority. The mind wants to generate it's own truth, not witness the universal one. It wants life to confirm whatever its current assumptions may be, even if they're full of inconsistencies. This includes the belief that it can predict the future, that we can know today what will make us happy tomorrow, and that you should have known better before a particular experience made you wiser.

Truth can never be attained through analysis. It's not a place at which you can arrive. It's always there, always present, revealing itself whenever you stop projecting meaning that isn't there. Whenever you feel instead of think. Whenever you observe without trying to control. This is why people often discover truth unexpectedly in the quiet moments contained in nature, in grief, in awe, in surrender. Silence is the doorway.

Truth reveals itself when you are embodied enough to resonate, still enough to hear its voice, and internal enough to keep the outside noise at bay. It does not require thought, yet it feels unmistakably right. As is the case with greater consciousness, you don't *find* truth. You stop resisting it and start letting it in.

Truth arrives the moment you stop interrupting life.

Letting go of subjective truths is rarely easy because it offers comfort the mind clings to, making it feels like it's doing its job of keeping you safe. That's also why the unknown feels so threatening, even though everything real lives there.

But once you connect with your body and start resonating with objective truth, a pivotal shift occurs: you stop fearing the unknown and start inhabiting it. You stop chasing happiness and start focusing on self-acceptance. You no longer get lost in time and start moving towards presence. The comfort zones of the past no long carry any pull—presence in the now does. Before you know it, your entire relationship to reality flips. The unknown becomes the field where truth appears, not the place where danger lurks.

Universal truth is not a philosophy. It is not a manifesto that someone, somewhere conjured up. It is the ethos of consciousness itself. It accompanies us into the material realm and imbues our physical being with energetic integrity—while being the sign post that points back to our spiritual essence so we can never really get lost.

Universal truth is simple, self-evident, and profoundly humbling. It dissolves ego the way light makes darkness disappear. The deeper the truth, the more your defenses fall away. In this context, humility emerges not as a virtue, but as alignment.

Once you taste the purity and simplicity of Universal law—once you experience the deep peace, trust, and flow contained within—there's no turning back. It's the way of the world. It's the design of life. It's waking up to the truth embedded in your bones.

This is when truth becomes the foundation for everything you do. And the changes are instantly noticeable. Decisions become obvious. Boundaries become natural. Your speech cleans itself up. Your attention becomes discerning. Your life gains traction, far more than you could ever imagine. Your orientation becomes steady. You stop fighting circumstances because you stop fighting reality itself.

Truth is where clarity, peace, and stability come together. It is the organizing principle of a conscious life. Without it, freedom has no purpose and love cannot mature. The human spirit fades when it has nowhere to go.

With truth, life begins to simplify.

Truth is not an endpoint—it is the entrance. It happens when matching what *is* with what is perceived. It opens your perception to a deeper intelligence governing everything. Truth is not the end of the journey but the beginning of an entirely new one—a life lived in synchronicity with what is, not in conflict with what you want it to be.

Truth is never about perfection. It's about being honest—first and foremost with yourself. You're not required to change your life overnight. You're just asked to stop lying to yourself long enough to see who you really are. From there, truth will guide you the rest of the way.

Chapter 4

Freedom

———◦———

Freedom is more essential than love. Love may stand as the supreme frequency, but it expands in the space that freedom creates.

Freedom is tightly linked to the evolution of the soul. It allows consciousness to explore itself through trial and error, expansion and collapse, to learn and become refined. It provides the petri dish for the contrast between living in alignment and living out of it. Without freedom, there would be no journey, no broadening of awareness, no eventual transcendence of form. Freedom is the space where self-realization unfolds.

There are four main phases a person experiences on their journey of self-realization: Belonging → Separation → Individuation → Transcendence

At first, you *belong*—to family, tribe, religion, or nation. In traditional or collectivist societies, people are deeply embedded within communal structures and responsibilities. These bonds offer continuity, but they often suppress individuation, autonomy, and the questioning of norms. Individual identity gets drowned out in favor of upholding the communal one, obscuring the deeper truth that the purpose of life is to outgrow identity altogether. The result is loyalty and conformity, but not necessarily awareness. And without developing a concept of *self*, there is little fuel for awakening—only compliance and devotion.

Then comes *separation*—usually through questioning, rebellion, or crisis. The soul must first become aware of itself as a distinct "I." This means confronting the most self-centric aspects of your personality, including desire, fear, ambition, and your definition of happiness. This phase can lead to friction within and without, as collective cultures often "cut down" anyone who rises too far above the group. But this is what spiritual growth and inner work are all about. Your strongest attachments become exposed so you can learn to let them go, and by experiencing the highs and lows of control can you tune into the frequency of surrender.

Next is *individuation*—the building of a self. Here, you test the power of your voice, the setting of personal boundaries, and your resilience to outside pressure. You no longer take everything you read as truth. Instead, you shape a self-image through discernment of what you stand for. This stage is not the end, but the necessary prelude to coming out of identity altogether. Without the self-image fully formed, its death is not possible.

Finally, there is *transcendence*—the conscious surrendering of attachment to your human form. True surrender is becoming an empty vessel, free of any judgment or repression. Many people raised in collectivist environments appear humble, yet their humility often stems from conditioning, not self-awareness. They think they're free, but compliance is not liberation.

Even decades of spiritual discipline do not guarantee the dismantling of identity.

Every soul must know itself as form before remembering its formless essence. Continued collectivism can delay this step. Individualism can accelerate it—but also trap you deeply in the addiction to personal power. All are part of the journey of self-realization. The discovery of one's own conscience is the doorway through which every soul must pass. Freedom is the backdrop that makes this possible.

True freedom requires minimal interference—enough structure for safety and fairness, but not so much that it dictates conscience. Spiritual evolution depends on the freedom to learn through consequence. Even when it creates some disorder, a society ultimately benefits when each person is allowed to make choices that reflect their current state of awareness.

There is no wisdom in asking individuals to abandon their inner authority for the sake of a manufactured collective ideal. A conscious society meets people where they are, instead of forcing them into sameness. When expression is restricted or dissent dismissed, the human spirit contracts. Over time, that contraction appears as depression, addiction, hopelessness, and despair. No culture thrives when its people cannot breathe.

Freedom reveals consequence and consequence teaches wisdom.

The distrust that elitist or authoritarian governments harbor toward freedom is simple: an unfree population requires governance. But when people are raised within a culture of personal responsibility, they learn to self-correct and grow their awareness—which is a direct threat to any regime built on fear and "protecting" people from themselves. Control may preserve a certain level of order, but too much suffocates the soul.

The idea of a world where every problem is solved on your behalf undermines the soul's evolution. The promise of safety without responsibility denies humanity the friction required for cultivating wisdom.

Ultimately, freedom is not just the liberty to act—it is the freedom *to be*. Not as systems define you, but as you actually are, so your evolution can unfold from truth instead of fear. No fair or conscious society has anything to fear from this state. This is how inner peace grows. And this is precisely why systems built on control are so invested in shaping the narrative. When life becomes centrally controlled, the risk is not political—it is spiritual: the dimming of human sovereignty at the very moment when consciousness is trying to expand.

CHAPTER 5

LOVE

For most people, love first appears as an experience between individuals. They think they "found" love in another person, or "lost" it when you drifted apart. They treat love as something that must be earned, reciprocated, or sustained through constant effort. But this is not love. This is the disconnected human trying to negotiate with their emotions, impose ever-changing boundaries, and practice conditional giving and receiving.

But love does not originate between two people. It is not romance, affection, shared experiences, or attachment. It is not even the acknowledgment from feeling seen and heard, or the beautiful ache of belonging you get from a tender embrace. Love is a field that emerges from being in a state of non-resistance to what is—a state of total absence of judgment. A love so consistent and persistent, so intricate and nuanced, it points to an artist who never rests to admire what he has done.

We honor life by participating in it.

As children, we long for love through our parents. As adults, we seek it through partners and children. But even in the most nurturing circumstances, love cannot be received from or given to another person. I can only be experienced through each others' orientation toward God Consciousness.

All things in nature—from trees to stone—offer no resistance. They let themselves be permeated by the passion for creation. They let it flow through them like the essential soul food that it is. It's only humans who complicate matters by getting in the way with their minds.

Your relationship with love is your ticket back home. The less you are attached to self, the greater you feel the pull. Love is the magnetism that reunites the Creator with the created. It's the energy that dissolves the limitations of form and reorients us towards Source.

This is why words spoken from God Consciousness contain no ill will. Why they radiate clarity and calm. Why others can sense authenticity in them.

This is why universal truth feels compassionate even when it's firm, and why lies feel empty even when they sound comforting. Love is not something you must bring to a situation. It is already contained in *all* situations.

Wherever reality is unobstructed, love is present.

Every spiritual tradition points to the same realization: love is not an emotion. It is the dominant vibration of an energetic universe. It is the rhythm of life, the intelligence that heals the body, and the depth that follows grief. It's a frequency that elevates all forms of existence to the same level of importance: the honor of having been created.

There is no lack of love in the world. There is just an absence of allowing it. The moment the mind gets lost in judgment, fear, comparison, resentment, or control, it severs the connection. This separation from love appears in the body as tension and in the mind as confusion. This is why even small acts of honesty, kindness, or surrender bring relief. In those moment you don't "receive" love. You simply stop withholding it from yourself.

Most suffering begins with the belief that we are separate from love.

The more love becomes obscured, the more fear steps in to govern. The mind takes over as the navigator of life, building belief systems for imagined security, identities to simulate belonging, and narratives to project stability. As felt connection fades, the natural intelligence of love gets replaced by imitation forms—attachment, avoidance, control, validation, need.

This withdrawal from love does not begin with ideology, culture, politics, or institutions. It begins in the human heart. The moment a person loses touch with God Consciousness, they lose the foundation upon which truth can play out and even freedom loses its purpose. Fear fills the vacuum, and what begins in one heart echoes outward into families, systems, nations—until the collective finds itself living inside a darkness it mistakes for reality.

In the Divine Architecture, truth orients you, freedom opens the space, and love is the radiance of reality when nothing is interfering with it. Since the beginning of civilization, this triad has formed the condition for the flowering of consciousness. And whenever it disappears from the human world, what remains is not a new foundation, but a reflection of just how much we've forgotten.

Part II

The Great Forgetting

CHAPTER 6

THE AGE OF INVERSION

Throughout history, evolution has always moved in the same rhythm: pushing into the unknown, testing what lies beyond the familiar, then preserving what proves true and sustainable. It stretches the boundaries of the possible, gathers information from the edge, and keeps only what can endure. Just as the seasons compel a tree to renew its strength, consciousness continually challenges its own truths to remain alive, healthy, and whole.

You can see this cycle play out in every generation. Youth naturally leans toward expansion: open, experimental, hungry for what lies beyond inherited belief. Elders lean toward conservation: they know what works and have little need to reinvent the wheel. As the young mature, they circle back to the fundamentals of life. What they once felt was restrictive, they now seek for grounding. What once seemed outdated becomes wise again.

The cycles of expansion and return are the heartbeat of evolution itself.

From time to time, creation stretches so far into experimentation that it begins to invert. Curiosity that once sought truth starts denying it, and the impulse for progress forgets what progress is for. What follows are eras where darkness is called light and chaos is seen as virtue—ages of inversion, when consciousness flips inside out and the collective mind loses its orientation to Source. Humanity is unquestionably passing through such an age now.

When inversion takes hold, clarity becomes suspicious. Naming the obvious is treated as abrasive—if not outright betrayal—because honesty threatens the collective trance. A culture of exaggerated sensitivity sweeps through the public sphere. Speaking plainly becomes obscene, often met with disproportionate consequences. Art withdraws and humor evaporates for fear of offense. Institutions elevate conformity over common sense. And the media insists, with growing confidence, that what you witness with your own eyes is not what is happening at all.

To those under hypnosis, inversion feels like progress. To the aware, it registers instantly as gaslighting. They watch a civilization spiral out of control while applauding the demolition of its own foundations. They understand that you should never discard natural law in the name of expanding material freedom. The resulting mass confusion is a kind of psychological vertigo in which everything familiar begins to blur and even sacred truths begin to wobble.

In an age of inversion, denying truth feels safer than facing it.

As a wave of groupthink sweeps across the world, some feel the dissonance but silence themselves to avoid being ostracized. Others are carried along by the current of collective hysteria. The pressure to conform becomes so pervasive that even leaders—once trusted to uphold truth—begin to mirror the madness. The human mind, disconnected from Spirit, can become infected just like the body. It starts replicating thought-forms that erode confidence in itself.

When this happens, the very qualities that sustain civilization—courage, discernment, humility, compassion—become distorted and even treated as offenses. Those who speak with clarity are labeled divisive, while those who perpetuate confusion are celebrated for "taking a stand." And the few who try to restore sanity find themselves ridiculed, attacked, or pushed to the margins. The mechanisms differ with each era, but the core pattern remains the same: censorship presents itself as truth-telling, and honesty is treated as a threat. A culture that cannot tolerate truth begins to police it.

None of this happens suddenly. Inversion builds quietly, often over generations. Institutions become captured and lose their integrity. Culture drifts from lived experience to managed perception through media. The farther society pulls from presence, the more it compensates with image and pretense. Meaning evaporates, replaced by virtue signaling. Ideology grows louder while wisdom grows faint. The mind, untethered from God Consciousness, begins to believe it can invent reality from scratch.

At the height of an inversion, reality turns fluid and certainty dissolves. What once felt stable feels negotiable. What was once obvious becomes debatable. And what should be sacred becomes optional. Even language becomes arbitrary and weaponized. Words cease to describe truth and begin to function as signs of allegiance. Ordinary people no longer trust what they're seeing with their own eyes. Public discourse—if it doesn't disappear altogether—becomes a circus. And political parties can suddenly represent the opposite of what they used to stand for. Leaders from all sectors—ever quick to seize the opportunity to expand their influence—mirror and amplify the mania without second thought. It's a bewildering state, one in which even deeply grounded individuals can momentarily lose their orientation.

CHAPTER 7

THE MANUFACTURING OF MIND

—◦—

One of the first systems to invert was education—the process by which mind-identification becomes a person's dominant operating system. Western, and now increasingly global, schooling rests on a single assumption: that the intellect is the highest function of a human being. From the moment you enter a classroom, the message is clear: head over heart, mind over body. Knowing replaces being. Thinking replaces listening.

Children enter school curious, intuitive, creative, and energetically open. They leave anxious, self-doubting, competitive, and deeply afraid of being wrong. What modern societies call "education" is really an initiation into a worldview where life is about planning, controlling, and proving yourself. And if you do that well, you'll survive. Going to school doesn't make you more excited about life. It shifts you from wonder to fear.

It's a system not designed to help you remember your essence, but to make you forget it. Instead of learning how to feel, trust, and create, you learn how to compare, comply, and please. Instead of discovering inner wisdom, you're taught to seek external validation. Instead of being shown that life naturally supports the aligned self, you're warned that life will punish you unless you get ahead. You go to bed each night fearing you'll never find happiness because others will beat you to it.

With that message comes a boatload of expectations. Grades, scores, assessments, benchmarks—these quickly become the framework of your identity. Children learn early on that mistakes are not learning opportunities, but blemishes on their record that will be held against them forever. That it's more important to pursue status than to do what you're passionate about. That it's not safe to show the normal confusion of teenage life, or else you might become labeled "not college-ready." This is not learning. It's identity manufacturing.

**Education stopped awakening minds
and started standardizing them.**

In such a world, the mind is not cultivated as a tool of creativity but conditioned to avoid punishment. The nervous system learns to live in threat detection rather than inspiration. Presence, intuition, emotional regulation, discernment—these are treated as extras.

Stillness, feelings, listening, and rest—no one teaches you that these form the foundation of a well-adjusted life. Instead, they're brushed off as soft skills, suitable only for those who are too weak for the real world. Consequently, the child learns to look for approval, constantly anticipating judgment.

Imagine if the message were as follows: *You are here to discover yourself through play and curiosity. Life supports you when you are honest with yourself. You have a unique contribution that unfolds through joy. You can do anything you feel called to do. There's no need to stress—you can trust yourself to respond to the future when it arrives.* What a different civilization that would create. But such a message would not produce obedient workers, predictable voters, or lifelong dependents on systems of authority. And so it is withheld.

Schooling no longer teaches you how to think—it teaches you what to think.

It's plain to see that modern education was not born from wisdom traditions but from the need to staff factories. It didn't evolve to raise consciousness but to ensure a steady flow of labor. Its model was industrial: efficiency, uniformity, hierarchy. The goal was never self-belief—only believing what you're told. The system doesn't ask, *Who are you?* or *What are you here to contribute?* It asks, *How well can you perform the task we've prepared for you?* And so, memorization was encouraged over reflection. Competition became more important than community. And obedience was rewarded, while critical thinking became labeled as *too risky*.

But it doesn't end there. The adult world mirrors the trend. Workplaces reward productivity. Politics rewards conformity. Media rewards outrage. Even religion, in many forms, rewards deference over self-realization. The same system continues. You graduate from one layer of conditioning to another, each promising freedom, while dragging you farther away from it.

Coming of age in this environment, most people have been trained so thoroughly to live in their heads that they can no longer imagine another way. They plan, calculate, analyze, and cope. They believe their thoughts, not their hearts. The result is a society of minds managing their existence rather than souls pursuing their purpose.

CHAPTER 8

GOVERNANCE WITHOUT GOD

You can tell what a society truly worships by how it understands authority. When people lose their connection to Source, they begin looking outward for guidance, safety, and structure. Into that vacuum steps the state, slowly assuming the role of moral parent—deciding what is safe, what is right, what is allowed. Laws multiply to fill the space where inner truth once lived. Citizens become conditioned to believe their rights are granted by government rather than inherent to their being. Few shifts reveal the difference between mind-identification and God Consciousness more clearly than this.

Fear quickly becomes the most efficient instrument of governance. Policies begin to embed it. Institutions expand to justify their own relevance. What initially appears as necessary structures gradually becomes a grid of control. Calls for compliance start to drown out critical thought. Obedience is praised as maturity. And genuine clarity—the one rooted in conscience—is quietly reframed as defiance.

In a world aligned with God Consciousness, unity rises naturally from each person's orientation toward objective truth. But in a de-spiritualized society, unity must be manufactured. Sameness replaces authenticity. Ideology substitutes for conscience. Personal development becomes a private hobby rather than a civic virtue. And in the absence of inner authority, the collective mind becomes a kind of substitute god—offering certainty to those afraid of the next thing they are told could go wrong. Group membership is marketed as safety, while those living from inner truth are cast into isolation.

Navigating life without a living connection to the divine isn't just difficult—it's destabilizing. It leaves societies vulnerable to overlords taking control precisely because individuals no longer trust their own clarity.

A population disconnected from truth becomes governable through fear.

Government keeps expanding until what was meant to flow through love begins circulating through rules and regulations. The state becomes the life-manager. Politicians grow their influence by rebranding control as responsibility, intelligence, and care. The more unpredictable they can make life feel, the easier it is to justify new systems to contain it.

Over time, the control structures become so internalized that people begin policing themselves—editing their words, curating their identities, and shrinking their truth long before anyone intervenes. Social pressure keeps everyone in line, and the fear of exclusion becomes the ultimate punishment.

Groupthink is not born of stupidity—it is born of the fear of standing alone, of being judged, of losing status with the tribe. When survival becomes tied to maintaining an image, authenticity grows too costly to sustain. People conform—not from conviction, but to avoid trouble. Ideas don't spread because they are true—they spread because they are safe to repeat.

In an effective tyranny, the prison inside the mind does most of the work. You know you're trapped when silence feels safer than honesty and obedience is seen as the highest character trait. You know you're being propagandized whenever governing bodies appeal to "safety" or "the greater good." These are all signs of a culture that has forgotten how to trust life.

Governance without God inevitably devolves into arbitrary lawmaking. Behind every ordinance lies a special interest. Behind every mandate, a benefactor. Behind every restriction, an incentive. Politics rarely serves truth. It serves the preservation of budgets, careers, and narratives. Markets self-correct because bad ideas fail. But bureaucracies rarely self-correct because they grow from failure—each failure becoming the rationale for more funding, more measures, more control. In such a system, emergencies are not disruptions—they are fuel.

It is no surprise, then, that crises appear endless—wars, panics, upheavals, each one reinforcing the machinery. Narrative control—backed by an army of hired "experts"—keeps the engine running. Facts are bent, inconvenient truths disappear, and history is rewritten to support the dominant story. Everything is curated to maintain the illusion of a coherent, benevolent, all-knowing state.

Nothing expands authority faster than crisis, and nothing threatens it more than clarity.

A culture obsessed with enforcing sameness produces citizens who are constantly on edge. Everything becomes amplified. Disagreement borders on hostility. Divergence is framed as betrayal. Even neutrality is seen as immoral. A calm, grounded presence becomes threatening in a society that demands constant virtue signaling.

In a mind-driven world, stillness is dangerous because it cannot be interpreted. Mystery is subversive because it cannot be measured. Creativity and independent action risk destabilizing the established order. And God Consciousness is shunned because it cannot be controlled. In such an environment, the ungoverned human—quiet, awake, inwardly free—is made to feel like an anomaly.

The mind insists that rights come from officials who draft bills into law. That they can be granted, revoked, negotiated, lobbied, and reframed in accordance with the mindset of the times. But rights rooted in God Consciousness do not exhibit such variability. They are considered inalienable—not because a piece of paper says so—but because they arise from the architecture of existence itself.

This is why the most destabilizing presence to an unguided government is not the activist, but the person who has remembered their essence. One who listens to conscience cannot be bribed. One who trusts life cannot be intimidated. One rooted in God Consciousness does not *believe* in freedom—they embody it. They do not wait for rights to be assigned—they express them. They do not look up to government—they look inward to God. A people capable of self-governance require very little law. A people governed by fear will need laws without end.

CHAPTER 9

THE RELIGION OF PROGRESS

————◆————

When a civilization loses touch with the sacred, it does not become less spiritual—it becomes spiritual in distorted and contradictory ways. Instead of surrendering through stillness, presence, and reverence, it gives itself over to noise, branding, and identity. Instead of experiencing purpose through flow and co-creation, it elevates shopping sprees, productivity hacks, and career ladders into rites of passage. Culture does not disappear when God is forgotten—it just becomes a shadow of itself. A civilization that has lost its foundation does not stop worshipping—it merely chooses new gods.

And so, progress became the ultimate deity. What began as a sincere desire to enhance life slowly grew into a movement to dominate it. On the surface, it sounds noble: innovate, achieve, move humanity forward. But hidden beneath is a darker belief—*life cannot be trusted, only planning can save us.* This is the pattern of every mind-identified society. Knowledge is idolized while prayer and communion are dismissed. Mental acuity vanquishes the unknown. Conformity to systems and procedures overtakes the quiet authority of living by your conscience.

When humanity tries to run the universe, it loses the experience of being part of it.

Culture, when detached from God Consciousness, turns every sacred impulse into a kind of spectacle. Art becomes entertainment. Language becomes marketing. Information becomes propaganda. Virtue becomes signaling. Outrage starts to feel meaningful. Celebrity replaces authenticity. Busyness feels like purpose. Ironically, the moment presence is lost, distraction from presence becomes the primary focus. A society cut off from inner peace becomes addicted to its own noise.

Nowhere is this more obvious than in the endless scrolling, reacting, and pretending that dominate the modern digital life. The mind, disconnected from Spirit, seeks constant stimulation to drown out silence. Even moments of intimacy become opportunities for validation. A barrage of opinions fills every channel—not to foster reflection, but to avoid truth. The modern mind cannot tolerate stillness because stillness exposes the emptiness inside.

As the noise amplifies, the self-absorbed mind shifts from "Is it true?" to "Who is watching?" Conscience fades away and consensus takes its place, enforced through fear of erasure. Cancel culture is not an anomaly—it is a symptom of a God-less world where forgiveness has become impossible. In such a world, the collective must continually find someone to condemn so it can feel righteous again.

In a world without conscience, punishment is the only ritual left.

In a disconnected society, even creativity loses its soul. True art is a dance with mystery—an intimate exchange with the formless as it becomes form. But when mystery is filtered through the mind alone, artists turn into content producers, spirituality becomes a lifestyle brand, and symbols lose their depth, collapsing into one-dimensional iconography. Culture may borrow the language of awakening, but it cannot tolerate the space for reflection that makes awakening real. Instead, it imitates transcendence while never moving beyond thought.

Progress, in its original form, was the impulse to evolve the things that matter, and leave behind the things that don't. But the progressive mind cannot rest—it requires a problem to justify its existence. If it cannot find one, it invents one. It makes rest feel irresponsible, and stillness feel wasteful. There must always be a goal to chase, for the mind to feel its own importance. And with every achievement comes a new deficiency to correct. In a God-less society, everything becomes urgently significant. You are pressured to work harder, focus longer, plan more precisely, and achieve more effectively. But the real fatigue isn't physical—it's spiritual. No mind-made system can replicate the intelligence of divine order.

Much of what flies under the banner of progress began with genuine care—a desire to protect the vulnerable or ease suffering. But without God Consciousness, the mind co-opts compassion to inflate its own self-image. It says, "I will heal you because I can," not "because we are one." Or, "I am virtuous because I take action," instead of "It is good to do good." True service requires no audience and no applause. You give because inwardly you are overflowing.

The progressive mind uplifts from superiority, not love.

The modern faith in progress insists that constant motion must be meaningful. As long as something is being investigated, optimized, or invented, we assume we're advancing. But spiritual evolution is not a forward march.

It isn't about getting somewhere—it's about learning how to *be* here, in unresisting presence with what already is.

Progress itself is not the issue. The problem is pursuing it without God Consciousness to give it a frame. Vast energy has been poured into systems of science, research, technology, and product development that offer no nourishment for the soul, and that only reinforce a sense of arrogance that we can improve life through control.

CHAPTER 10

THE ECONOMY OF ILLUSION

Every collapsing civilization shares a simple pattern: its economy stops reflecting reality and begins producing and monetizing illusion. When connection to Source fades, the market no longer follows the intelligence of life—it follows the anxiety of disconnection. Value stops being created from truth and starts being extracted from fear. What arises is not an economy built to serve human flourishing, but one that amplifies human insecurity. People work not to co-create, but to protect themselves from imagined loss. Scarcity becomes the organizing principle, and lack the root motivation.

If you've ever wondered why the world feels so rushed, it's because a system built on fear can never rest. It must keep moving and accelerate endlessly. It keeps everyone panicking and reacting—because if you slow down long enough to actually see what's happening, you might wake up from the illusion.

This does not mean you're supposed to reject the material world. It means you're supposed to engage in it with God Consciousness. When you do, exchange becomes an act of mutual uplift—simple, honest, regenerative. Value finds its natural flow, and money returns to its rightful function as a token of trust, a symbol of shared intention, carrying the frequency of both giver and receiver.

In the hands of an unconscious mind, however, currency becomes a tool for domination, self-importance, and proof of worth. Subsequently, trust dissolves, and money ceases to represent a blessing. The illusion economy insists you can buy your way into safety and happiness—shifting society from alignment-centered to acquisition-driven. Life becomes a forced, materialistic exchange that keeps broad swaths of the population asleep.

The more people forget their inherent enoughness, the more they compete for validation in material form.

Scarcity is the first lie—the idea that there is not enough. Not enough time, not enough money, not enough safety, not enough freedom. Anxiety becomes profitable because anxious minds don't awaken—they comply, consume, and stay trapped in a low-grade survival state. Yet nothing about scarcity is natural. The sun does not charge for its light. Trees do not invoice the soil. Life is designed to support mutual growth. Abundance is not a luxury. It is the baseline of all existence.

The mind, however, only perceives lack, never what is already given. Scarcity is nothing more than conditioned thinking that blocks the natural flow of abundance. It is not a material reality. And it feeds on itself: the more you chase wealth, the poorer you feel.

A disconnected mind cannot see the infinite abundance available to all life forms. Its lens is too narrow, too busy scanning for threats. Add to it the barrage of marketing and propaganda by those who control the airwaves, and you can see why the constant fear-mongering is not an accident. Once people believe resources are limited, they will stay in line and uphold the system in hopes of getting their slice of the imaginary pie.

When the prevailing attitude is *What if something goes wrong?* fear becomes the dominant currency. Entire industries monetize this dread—insurance, security, surveillance, pharmaceuticals, advertising, politics. Fear sells protection by first convincing you that you are unsafe. It makes you guard things you don't have and defend identities that aren't real. It promises safety while deepening dependence. In this way, governments, corporations, and ideologies all sell variations of the same illusion: *Surrender your freedom, and we will protect you from life itself.* It is the perfect inversion of spiritual truth, where life is never the enemy—only a gift you are being asked to accept.

When an economy forgets truth, it starts selling fear.

Debt is the next evolution of the illusion. Mortgages, loans, and credit cards turn your entire life into a repayment schedule. You're not working for money—you're trading your vitality to service interest. You borrow against the future to sustain a present built on illusion. Debt is modern feudalism disguised as empowerment. The system isn't offering you jobs as much as it wants your preoccupation. And the more you remain trapped in survival mode, the less space there is for presence, creativity, or the experience of what's actually real.

Career is the peak of the ladder. Labor was once participation in creation—a way to give shape to divine will. But in the mind-identified state, work stops being devotion and becomes self-preservation. People no longer work to serve life—they work to survive it, manage it, and control it. Anyone who interferes with their ability to make ends meet becomes a threat. Everyone is either for you or against you.

When your output determines your worth, exhaustion is seen as a badge of honor. Logging in at midnight is proof of dedication. The more depleted you are, the more "responsible" you feel. You can never admit to taking rest—it looks suspiciously like you're not doing enough. And so, you spend your whole life earning the right to retire, and once you get there, you feel guilty for doing nothing. It's a kind of cultural insanity.

At the energetic level, work without joy is violence against the soul. It drains not just your energy but your dignity. The endless race to produce more, earn more, achieve more is not progress—it's a distortion of your purpose. You came here to experience flow and participate in the communion of co-creation, not to grind yourself into dust.

Inevitably, advertising becomes the heart of this system, repeating the same message in infinite variations: *you are almost enough.* Just one purchase away, one improvement away, one fix away. Temporary dopamine hits keep the wheel spinning, but fulfillment is never allowed to fully arrive—because if it did, the entire structure would collapse. The illusion economy cannot coexist with one that fosters enlightenment. It depends on restlessness, on not-enough-ness, on constant consumption. It depends on people who fear themselves and their futures. In such a model, truth is nowhere to be found.

CHAPTER II

SCIENCE WITHOUT SOUL

Science at its best is a method of inquiry. At its worst, it becomes a replacement religion. In a world cut off from God Consciousness, mental acuity displaces a deeper reverence for life, peer review replaces inward reflection, and appointed experts become the new arbiters of truth. This happens, not because science is inherently malicious, but because a mind disconnected from Source must worship something—and it inevitably gravitates toward whatever promises certainty.

In truth, science and spirituality were never meant to be adversaries. One studies creation from the outside, the other from the inside. One focuses on observable and measurable rules and behaviors, the other listens for the intelligence behind it. But somewhere along the way, the modern world embraced the notion that what cannot be defined does not exist. If the soul cannot be represented as a chart or graph, it must be imaginary. If consciousness cannot be dissected, it must be a neurological glitch. If the divine cannot be analyzed, it must be myth.

Ironically, the same scientific establishment that once mocked ancient cultures for believing in invisible forces now describes reality in terms of fields, frequencies, and nonlocal intelligence. Yet even quantum physics, which hints so openly at the presence of a deeper order, still finds itself avoiding the broader implications. The equations are accepted, but the ultimate truth they point to is denied. And the reason is simple: recognizing truth requires a degree of humility that only comes from personal surrender—something the mind alone cannot manufacture.

A consciousness-first universe leaves no room for human supremacy.

When left to itself, the mind does what it always does: it narrows the focus, amplifies the parts it understands, and dismisses whatever it cannot label or finds inconvenient. This is not a flaw of science itself—many scientists know the limits of their method—but the result is a worldview built on partial understanding.

And when this partial understanding is co-opted by industries and political powers for the purpose of commerce and social control—when half-truth is sold as certainty—science drifts from inquiry into dogma. It stops exploring the unknown and begins enforcing answers to protect its own status. Funding pressures create consensus. Data replaces wisdom. The laboratory becomes a kind of temple—run by people who view consciousness as a byproduct of the brain and the universe as a random accident with no author. What they cannot grasp is that truth is not found by denying mystery, but by working with it, welcoming it, embracing it. Without true humility, science becomes an instrument of manipulation—used to further the interests of those who control the grants pipeline.

You can tell where the funding comes from when science seeks to dominate rather than create harmony. When it treats nature as machinery to be engineered, owned, and improved. When the human body becomes a transportation device prone to malfunctioning. When emotions are reduced to chemical imbalances. When death becomes a medical failure that can be avoided. When health becomes all about compliance with protocols. In this worldview, a human being is no longer a sacred container through which life forces flow, but a biological apparatus to be tracked, optimized, and updated. Nothing sovereign. Nothing holy. Nothing whole.

This is why modern medicine looks for symptoms, not cures. It does not believe in causes deeper than chemistry. Health campaigns tell you to fear sunlight while promoting synthetic foods. The immune system is treated as an adversary to be subdued. Doctors prescribe weight-loss pills instead of exercise. Psychiatry names disorders faster than it can heal them—while unable to acknowledge the root of most suffering: the disconnection from Source. It's a tell-tale sign of a spiritually bankrupt science when it pathologizes creation itself.

CHAPTER 12

THE TECHNOLOGICAL DELUSION

———◦———

When a civilization loses sight of the Source, it looks for meaning in its own creations—unaware that the mind can only build things that reflect its own confusion.

Among all technological revolutions, artificial intelligence is the most revealing. It reflects the unconscious attempt to construct an all-knowing God, a system that sees everything, knows everything, predicts everything. One that is always listening, ready to fulfill your biggest desires and dispel your deepest fears.

But omniscience without conscience does not produce wise algorithms. It can only lead to a more tightly engineered control grid—one where surveillance is sold as safety, information becomes decoupled from its context, and data is used to alter reality

Technology itself is not the problem.
Technology without soul is.

In its relentless drive to dispel the unknown, the unconscious mind becomes obsessed with innovation. The constant replacement of what *is* keeps society from experiencing the deeper knowing that arises from letting things be.

The awakened human, however, recognizes the obvious limitations of systems that can calculate fast yet cannot care at all. Speech programs can replicate language, but they cannot articulate intuition. Chatboxes can mimic compassion, but they cannot actually feel it. A machine can store knowledge, but it cannot embody truth. After all, it has no body. It possesses no sensations, no inner resonance through which truth reveals itself. At best, it imitates the brain. But it can never transmit the energy of presence.

Can AI compete with—and even surpass—human skill at the surface level of reality? Almost certainly. Can it access the deeper realm of God Consciousness? Not at all. For any machine to become truly sentient, it would require a biological structure capable of feeling, integrating, and surrendering—an entire nervous system softened through suffering, expanded through love, and refined through inner spaciousness. It would need the capacity to be still so that truth can arise from within its cells. It would need the ability to hold space for life, not merely process information about it.

AI can only reflect the collective state of consciousness—never exceed it.

The data scientists and engineers at the forefront of developing AI are humans. The data they aggregate is from humans. The way AI learns is from humans. It doesn't gain insight from mystery. It doesn't pull from the unknown. It doesn't train itself to trust and be in receiving mode. It compiles itself on the current state of humanity—flaws and all.

Ultimately, AI is nothing more than the amplification of human conditioning. It's algorithms include all the wounds, biases, and projections of a deeply flawed and unhealed species and then reflects them back, scaled and organized by computational power. Perhaps this can lead to some insights about one's issues. But then AI is little more than a talking electronic journal.

The real danger does not come from the machines themselves. It comes from how we stop evolving ourselves. The more we let technology predict our choices, the more we stop listening for what's true. The more it remembers for us, the more we stay stuck in the past. The more it speaks for us, the more we repeat what we already know. The more processes become automated, the less people cross paths to remind each other of their common humanity. Consciousness evolves through direct experience with uncertainty, contrast, stillness, and the unexpected—none of which can be programmed. The more frictionless life becomes, the more your inner being loses the tension that shapes it and makes it grow.

No human has ever awakened through convenience.

The real progress trap is not that artificial intelligence will become conscious, but that human beings will stop encountering the very circumstances that challenge them to question their truth. To assess what works and what doesn't. To feel the need to take control of their destiny. The hidden cost of programs running the world is that it erodes your participation in the unfolding of life. When systems anticipate your needs and plan your path, you no longer have to show up and meet the moment yourself. And as engagement decreases, discernment atrophies. Efficiency may rise, but resonance—the embodied sense of truth that comes only through lived experience—begins to wither and the human is soon an empty shell.

Inner wisdom does not awaken in isolation. It awakens through contact with life. Even the deepest insights from sitting on a meditation cushion do not crystallize until you move back into the world. The body needs to feel the texture of its own aliveness, the contrast of desires not met, the pulse of the earth beneath your feet, and the rhythm of new moments arriving to register what is real. It comes to life when experience is vivid enough for truth to travel through the senses and settle into a felt knowing.

Technology can simulate knowledge, but it cannot co-create with Source.

Technocracy is the political expression of a world ruled by data, efficiency, and optimization—values that become directionless the moment they are severed from Spirit. It treats human beings not as embodied souls but as configurable units to be managed, arranged, and assigned to keep the machine running. A society disconnected from God Consciousness inevitably drifts into rule by elites—whereas a society rooted in it becomes capable of governing itself. This is why technocratic systems fear silence—because in silence, people remember they were born free.

CHAPTER 13

GENDER, IDENTITY & THE BODY

———◦———

When a soul first arrives in a human body, there is no identity—only being. But as mental conditioning takes hold, the body is seen as the *self*, and becomes the focal point of the mind's confusion. *Why do I look this way? Why do I feel this way? Why can't I be different?* You get pulled into the thinking that your body holds the answer to *Who am I?*

In a mind-driven world, no one tells you that you're an infinite being—and that it takes time for your soul to adjust to the limitations and sensitivities of a body. That it's normal to struggle trying to fit your formless essence into a physical container. That your physique will continue to change its shape and function. And that any efforts to conform it to external ideals or internal sentiments are an endless battle.

Attachment to the body keeps you in a state of eternal unrest.

Any crisis around gender, identity, and bodily modification is not a problem of biology but of disconnection. The more disconnected a culture is from God Consciousness, the more it tries to fix itself through form. This is why so many feel estranged inside their own skin. Instead of simply inhabiting the body, it becomes something that carries the full weight of how you see yourself and how you want to be seen. Any confusion or judgments in your self-image, you try to rectify by re-sculpting your physical shape. The mind begins obsessing about the exterior in hopes of restoring a sense of inner authenticity.

But this is the core misunderstanding of the modern age: believing truth can be attained by modifying your appearance. The mind assumes, *If I change the outside, the inside will finally settle down.* Science, technology, and the marketplace are quick to seize the opportunity to amplify the discontent. Yet no lasting peace can come from the outside-in. Identity built on looks is incredibly fragile—constantly shifting and never enough. As long as how you feel depends on how you're seen, you will never be at home in your body.

None of this makes the struggle wrong. Those who wrestle with gender, self-image, or embodiment are not broken—they stand at the very edge of the tension between their human form and formless essence. This is the sacred terrain where transcendence can take place—where peace can be attained by learning to hold everything as true. Those whose lifestyles fit more neatly into cultural norms will find themselves challenged to go there in other ways.

The body is not the enemy. It is a temporary vessel that can guide you through all lessons of life—if only you pause to listen. When someone feels misaligned with their vessel, the issue isn't that the body is wrong—it's that the connection to what animates the body has dimmed.

When that connection goes quiet, the outer form grows unbearably loud. Awkwardness, separateness, and confinement become the dominant experience. The mind compensates by constructing a self-image around labels, pronouns, aesthetics, and procedures in an effort to recover a sense of self it can accept. But an identity held together by thought is as fickle and unstable as the mind that produces those thoughts.

**When the light within dims, the body
starts shouting for recognition.**

In contrast, God Consciousness takes you out of your *self*. It doesn't compel you to seek validation, reinforcement, or explanation from anyone about who you are. Nor does it require you to generate it from within. You simply *are*. Everything simply *is*.

It's important to acknowledge that there is real suffering here. Many live with deep pain, confusion, and alienation from their own bodies—often since childhood. They deserve compassion, not made to feel misguided. But compassion is not the same as agreement. It is possible to honor someone's experience while still naming the deeper disconnect beneath it. True compassion can hold space for pain while still speaking with clarity.

Ultimately, forming an identity is part of everyone's evolution. It can be seen as a necessary bridge, but not as a permanent resting place. Letting go of form identity represents the core challenge of our journey of self-realization. In this age of inversion, we are witnessing the collapse of identification itself, not just a reshuffling of labels.

No one is born into the wrong body, but many are born into the wrong *belief* about the body. Life chooses each form with precision—not for ease, comfort, or even physical prowess—but for curriculum. Some bodies feel like home. Others feel like rejection. Both are teachers of transcendence.

The more society disconnects from Source, the more it tries to create meaning through material modification—tattoos, surgeries, digital avatars, curated looks. These are not signs of vanity but symptoms of spiritual amnesia. The surface is being used to make up for what the interior has forgotten. But moral judgment, political force, or cultural shaming offer no solution. The only sustainable resolution is a return to God Consciousness. When alignment returns and awareness reconnects, attachment to the body as identity softens. Your physical shape stops being the place where your sense of self lives and becomes a vessel again—not perfect, not permanent, but enough for while you're here.

CHAPTER 14

THE CULT OF HEALTH

———◆———

When a culture is ruled entirely by the mind, the body is no longer honored as a vessel for sacred consciousness—it becomes an object to manage and control. Nowhere is this more visible than in how a society approaches health.

Instead of building awareness around the body's inherent desire to be balanced, self-sustaining, and self-healing, modern notions of health are a marketplace of fear, obsession, and biohacking. Instead of being guided by the inner intelligence from which all well-being flows, most people are consumed by surface matters. Which gym you belong to, which protocol you're on, which influencers you're following. Amidst all this effort and expenditure, the real focus isn't even your health. The top concern is how you look and appear to others. Health has been reduced to a subscription model, a lifelong dependency on a machine disguised as self-care. The body is no longer a temple—it's a problem that needs to be fixed to uphold your personal brand.

In a de-spiritualized world, the medical system no longer asks, *What is the body trying to communicate?* It asks, *How can we mute the symptoms enough to continue working, consuming, and complying?* A society that worships the mind treats discomfort as a malfunction instead of a signal that something is off. Illness is not seen as a wakeup call to recalibrate, but as an interruption of your busy schedule.

True healing requires getting in touch with yourself in a way that is too slow, too personal, too intimate for the modern person's mental, emotional, and physical constitution. Moreover, it threatens the money pipeline that feeds medical schools, doctors, hospitals, the pharmaceutical industry, and government agencies. Focusing on treatment of symptoms is faster, much more profitable, and turns people into lifelong customers.

The real tragedy of the sickness loop is that people no longer trust their own bodies—which are home to their wisdom. Instead, they are taught to fear sensations, to pathologize emotions, and to interpret their biology purely through diagnostic tests rather than direct experience. Medical examination has its place, but should only serve to help build a deeper, more honest relationship with one's physical being.

Ultimately, our form is never the issue. Disconnection is. When mind, body, and spirit are aligned, your body speaks for itself. It asks for sunlight, hydration, nutrition, rest, exercise, and alerts you to any changes in habit or toxins in your environment. Even your heart aches for attention or your lungs express grief when there is a need for emotional care.

But when you're operating from your head, you don't listen to this intelligence. It feels almost too simple. You see yourself as a bigger problem that needs complex solutions. You believe rest is irresponsible and that feeling stressed is a sign your life is going somewhere. And when wear and tear arises, you blame your body for not holding up, and ask your doctor to prescribe a pill to make it go away. You avoid stillness and the deeper inquiry of what your body needs to maintain the state of true well-being.

Modern medicine completes the split from God Consciousness by cutting people off from their bodies.

Medicine without reverence sees isolated organs, not an interconnected chain of energy. It thinks the body is activated by chemistry, not animated by consciousness. It focuses entirely on data and sanctioned protocols, without considering divine design.

The unique, dynamic, soulful being that you are is relegated to statistical averages and numbers on a chart.

As if blood pressure, cholesterol, weight, and glucose levels can quantify the mystery of life and be fixed through intervention. That doesn't mean those indicators don't have some value, but you see them very differently through the eyes of God Consciousness than through the conditioned mechanics of the mind.

Ultimately, no scan can identify the intelligence that provides directives to your cells. No lab can detect the vibration of trust, grief, forgiveness, or purpose you carry. Practicing presence that heals does not appear in bloodwork and releasing stuck energy is nowhere to be found in mainstream medical journals. And so the system dismisses what it can't understand as nonexistent. It manages the body like an economy, where the goal becomes productivity, not vitality. People are kept alive so they can function, not so they can thrive.

A society that measures well-being in lifespan rather than aliveness thinks that survival alone is success.

This distortion becomes unmistakable when you look at the most basic element of sustenance: food. The body was designed to heal through nourishment, yet an entire civilization no longer sees nutrition as medicine. Meals are scheduled around work, not body type. Portions far exceed what is actually needed. Food becomes entertainment, status, distraction—anything but communion between the physical and the divine. Grocery aisles smell like chemistry labs, with bright packaging that disguises what's inside. The simple truth that the body thrives on what comes from the earth has been buried by the marketing of special-interest "science." Those who have the means to buy organic food are charged a premium for wanting what is natural, and even that label is under constant threat of manipulation.

A spiritually aware culture would teach children that the quality of food shapes the quality of thought. It affects how at home you feel in your body. It nourishes your connection to heart and soul. It has a direct impact on your ability to sit still and focus. Every grain, fruit, and seed carries sunlight, soil, and cosmic memory. To eat consciously is to remember where you come from.

Instead, children are raised on sugar, dyes, and preservatives—then medicated for the agitation their food created. Adults chase diets while starving themselves for minerals, suppress their appetite while craving a deeper connection, and count calories without ever asking why they eat when they're lonely. The modern food crisis is not merely biological—it's existential.

People who forget how to feed themselves have already forgotten who they are.

The result is a world where constant doctor visits are considered normal, radiant vitality is rare, and healing is seen as a miracle rather than the body's natural state. People die slow internal deaths, not because the body is failing, but because the connection to the body has been severed. The real illness is alienation from our divine design.

A whole human being requires so very little: nourishment, stillness, movement, sunlight, truth. These are simple, ancient foundations—yet they are the first things a disconnected civilization forgets. In a world built on control, remembering that the body already knows how to heal becomes a quiet act of rebellion—one that a mind-dominated age cannot tolerate.

CHAPTER 15

THE FRACTURED FAMILY

The family is the smallest system of spiritual incubation—a self-governing container where human awareness can be shaped, guided, protected, and matured. Before a person encounters schools, institutions, or the workplace—before they become aware of the outside world—they experience the family. It's the first environment where you learn what it means to exist in a body, form an identity, relate to others, and develop a conscience.

That is why, in every era where societies become more mind-driven, the family is the first institution to weaken or dissolve. Not because progress demands it, but because the family is the last structure capable of producing sovereign individuals—people with enough inner grounding to resist psychological manipulation, social engineering, and state-manufactured fear. A strong family produces a strong conscience. A fractured family produces a fractured self. And nothing suits a self-serving government more than citizens who feel rudderless, ashamed, uncertain, and alone.

The family and the state are, by nature, incompatible sources of authority. One cultivates order from the inside out, while the other manages behavior from the outside in. A child whose conscience is nurtured at home does not need the state to act as a moral parent, and they naturally move into the world with confidence and presence. A child who never develops a conscience is easily governed, and their lack of trust in life keeps them small and compliant. A government without soul has every incentive to keep the family fractured.

And so, as the administrative state grows, the family becomes the ultimate target. Institutional expansion, bureaucratic "compassion", and constant crisis management don't seek to destroy it outright, but hollow it out enough until it loses its function and moral authority. That has been the trajectory since the start of the 20th century: children removed from their parents through compulsory schooling, multi-generational communities dissolved by industrial migration to urban environments, mothers pulled from the home under the banner of liberation, fathers displaced and made to feel replaceable, and elders checked into institutions instead of honored as keepers of wisdom.

When the family weakens, the state strengthens.

Mind-identified systems disguise their efforts to control by branding them as freedom. In this way, the breakdown of the family was marketed as modernity, opportunity, and equality. Women were told that motherhood is "not enough," that home life is limiting, and that real power means joining the workforce. Men were told that their energy is toxic, that traditional roles are oppressive and obsolete. Children were told that experts know better than their parents. Elders were painted as burdens. Family became optional, replaceable, even regressive.

Of course, every one of these narratives contained a partial truth, which is why they worked. Yes, some women were confined. Yes, some men were abusive. Yes, some homes were unjust. But instead of healing the dysfunction, the solution presented was to replace the structure entirely. Instead of elevating the quality of fatherhood and motherhood, social and economic institutions—backed by the state—took over the function of both.

The most effective way to collapse the family was not to attack it directly, but to make single-income households impossible. When the economic system requires two adults to work full-time just to survive, the "choice" for women to work is no longer a choice—it becomes a necessity. Feminism, industrialization, taxation, and state expansion converged into the reality of today, where children spend more waking hours with nanny institutions than with blood relatives. Grandparents are shipped off to assisted living facilities, taking with them the depth of years, the patience of time, and the gratitude for the miracle of being alive.

This was not an accident but an authority transfer. By monopolizing media narratives, the state positions itself as the new arbiter of parenting. Grants and legislation signal markets to create products and services that reinforce the shift. NGOs promote the new story. Teachers are positioned as truth-tellers. Peers become the new emotional reference point. But a child raised by so many systems is, in effect, raised by none.

The quiet campaign against fatherhood was also not coincidental. True masculinity is not dangerous because it is violent—it is dangerous because it is sovereign. A grounded man—anchored, disciplined, and devoted to protecting what is sacred—cannot be controlled. Nowhere is this sovereignty more visible than in fatherhood. The state does not fear men with jobs or hobbies—it fears fathers. A father who lives by conscience is a firewall against tyranny. He will not comply with a system that violates truth and the sanctity of his family.

Unable to eliminate men outright, culture weakened the masculine role instead. It diffused fatherhood through distraction—addictions, entertainment, endless busyness—and then labeled any resistance to this erosion as "toxic." The result is a society full of males but few men, full of biological fathers but few protectors, and full of relationships but few partnerships rooted in conscience.

The feminine, meanwhile, was industrialized. Women were encouraged to imitate the most exhausted aspects of masculinity rather than embody the restorative strengths of the feminine: intuition, nurture, emotional intelligence, devotion, and embodied love. Millions now carry both responsibilities—career and family—with neither getting the full attention that it deserves. The modern woman was told she could "have it all," but what that actually meant was "do it all."

A society that undervalues motherhood always ends up spiritually malnourished.

A child needs three elements to form a coherent self: a steady masculine presence that models strength connected to conscience, a steady feminine presence that models love connected to truth, and a unified environment where the two cooperate rather than compete. Remove any one of these, and the child still develops—but now through wounding instead of wisdom. This is why trauma, not inner guidance, has become the primary teacher in modern life. What the family once transmitted—values, belonging, purpose—is now left to public policies, counseling, and pharmaceuticals. The child is not just under-parented—they are *over-managed* by systems incapable of love.

The family, in its ideal form, is a field of conscious alignment—but in an age ruled by the mind, it becomes one of the first structures to splinter. Once the family weakens, identity blurs, authority dissolves, dependence rises, and the state fills the vacuum.

But no institution built without God Consciousness can hold what the family once held. The state cannot nurture. Markets cannot protect. Science cannot provide meaning. Technology cannot convey true belonging. A civilization cannot outsource the raising of a human being without losing the human being in the process.

CHAPTER 16

THE ILLUSION OF FREEDOM

Freedom in a de-spiritualized world is little more than choosing the flavor of one's confinement. You may choose from a variety of lifestyles, curated forms of self-indulgence, and endless material offerings. But spiritually, this is not freedom—that's choosing between options preselected by a system whose motives you never stopped to question.

You think you're free, yet you cannot step outside the machine that demands your life energy to afford that thought. You may "speak your mind," but only within the sanctioned boundaries of acceptable speech. You may "be whoever you want," so long as you remain marketable, manageable, and safely disconnected from presence. Is this better than overt bondage? Perhaps. But not by much. Personalization inside captivity is still captivity.

Real freedom begins with a single realization: you are 100% responsible for your own happiness. That's not a cynical statement in response to having been let down by life. Rather, it's a deep recognition that your life experience reflects your internal state—how you trust, how you love, how abundant you feel, how free you are. True freedom is the state of being inwardly uncompromised, anchored in conscience, obedient only to the natural law evident in reality itself.

As long as how you feel depends on your environment, you are not free.

The mistake of our age is to think that collapsing traditional structures means liberation. That conserving the truth means going backwards—when what it actually means is reconnecting to depth and truth that make life meaningful here and now. Nobody is saying to carry forward structures that may have existed in the past that themselves didn't honor these principles.

When the anchors of family, faith, and higher purpose dissolve, people do not become freer—they become easier to steer. Untethered from God Consciousness, the mind grows frantic and programmable. Governments and institutions step in and offer to save you. They promise you *limitless choice with no consequences, absolute autonomy with emotional cushioning, and a perpetual safety net.* If that sounds too good to be true, that's because it is. When the state announces measures "for your own good," what it's really plotting is to take away your sovereignty.

Freedom is not the right to avoid the discomfort required for growth. It is living in honest relationship with yourself, your feelings and circumstances, and acting from the clarity of your conscience. Then no outside power can threaten your capacity to distinguish mind projection from connected reality. Only when that capacity is compromised does the mind reach outward for rescue.

Spiritually illiterate cultures will always think freedom means comfort and certainty. But it's really just sedation. Totalitarianism seldom arrives with banners or megaphones—it slips in when awareness has grown too tired from the mental exhaustion of living in a spiritual vacuum. The more a population retreats into managed living, programmed safety, and consuming consensus-approved content, the weaker the inner faculty becomes that once made external regulation ineffective and unnecessary. Under such conditions, surveillance does not expand because citizens are dangerous, but because they are empty and disconnected from the consciousness that governs itself.

The mind that has not surrendered to divine order is compelled to manufacture its own.

As the sovereignty of individuals gets hollowed out, the system becomes further inclined to treat everyone the same. Eventually, equality becomes the benchmark that replaces the illusion of freedom, because sameness is even easier to manage.

But no two human beings are the same. Each of us arrives with a distinct level of awareness, a unique set of lessons, a specific divine blueprint, and our own path of self-realization. We differ in temperament, gifts, passions, and intelligence. To insist that all humans are "equal" ignores the infinite diversity built into creation itself.

Do some people appear to benefit from being born at a certain time, with certain resources, into certain circumstances? Perhaps. But those who see life through God Consciousness understand that those individuals will be tested in their own ways, challenged to grow in their own time, often by exactly those seemingly advantageous conditions.

You cannot look at anyone from the outside and declare their life to be easier or harder, fairer or unfair. Every person is experiencing reality according to the extent of their inner awareness. Every life is tailored for that soul's growth. Advantages bring their own challenges, just as hardships bring their own forms of strength.

That doesn't mean one shouldn't help to change lives. But it also means you see the experience each soul is seeking to have, and how everyone manifests the circumstances that attract the lessons they must learn. Divine timing is not an arbitrary force looking down from above. It is the mirror of life reflecting back all the ways in which you have not yet remembered your wholeness.

Freedom suffocates when individuality is diminished to avoid offense or friction.

True freedom does not require permission or complex laws. It simply requires clarity of conscience. It is not granted by governments, guaranteed by courts, or achieved by activism. It is a vibrational state in which action flows from awareness, not fear. A person who is internally free may be censored, rejected, or imprisoned, yet their trust in truth remains untouchable. A person who is internally enslaved may possess every right and luxury in the world and still live as a hostage to their mind. The mind seeks freedom from limits. Spirit wants you to be free so you can live with truth.

Elites often insist that ordinary people cannot be trusted to know what's good for them. But this attitude denies individuals the chance to learn and grow through lived experience—an essential part of consciousness unfolding.

Freedom descends into chaos only when it's separated from responsibility. A culture in which enough people are rooted in inner authority creates the stability required for everyone to live freely, each according to the stage of their journey.

When freedom is thought to be granted by others, it is already lost.

The greatest illusion of freedom isn't found in what we pursue—it's found in what we avoid. Enter the modern safety industry with its favorite instrument: fear. Today's world has perfected the art of selling protection—be it financial, medical, digital, or emotional. You buy insurance just in case something catastrophic happens, unaware that you're wagering that it *will*, while the insurer is wagering that it *won't*.

But the more you fixate on safety nets, the more vulnerable you feel. That's how energy works. Whatever you give your attention to grows. The fear you try to solve by purchasing endless policies intensifies. The money you save to feel secure makes you feel poorer. The relationships you maintain to avoid loneliness deepen your isolation. The career you cling to for stability makes you feel even more lost. By focusing on what you don't want, you breathe life into it.

The more you guard against loss, the less you live. New chapters can't enter when you cling to structures that once protected you, but no longer serve you. Growth cannot happen when you refuse to let an outdated version of yourself die. Renewal never arrives while you keep the expired parts of your life—relationships, identities, beliefs, careers—on life support.

When you keep reviving what's meant to end, exhaustion becomes inevitable.

Risk management industries feed on your subconscious fear of endings. They sell compassion to mitigate what is simply your fear of letting go. Anti-aging products promise immortality. Pharmaceuticals sell endless equilibrium. Insurance policies promise protection from every possible threat.

But endings are only cruel when you demand permanence from a life that is anything but. Your deeper wisdom knows that a healthy detachment is the essential ingredient of flow and that every ending is a portal—life removing what your consciousness has already outgrown.

Every ending carries the seed of a truer beginning—but only for those willing to let the old dissolve. False safety nets keep you bound to the familiar while promising protection from the natural rhythm of renewal. A mind-identified world wants you to plan, insure, archive, accumulate—anything to avoid change. It urges you to drown out the quiet knowing that the river never rewards those who build walls around it, but those willing to step into the current, even when it means some things get swept away.

CHAPTER 17

THE CRISIS OF FAITH

Living with God Consciousness simplifies your life. It brings clarity where you were once confused, presence where anxiety once lived, and an inner authority that guides your choices without doubt or force. It helps you savor the moment, trust your own alignment, and remain composed through life's most challenging circumstances. Yet this simplicity carries a paradox: the more light you embody, the more darkness you inevitably see.

Once your inner vision clears, the outer landscape reveals itself—sharply, unmistakably. You witness how people harm themselves and each other through blind, mind-driven behavior. You see nations traumatizing their own citizens through senseless conflict. You see institutions—schools, media, medicine, science—operating without conscience, guided not by integrity but by extraction. You see millions working in jobs that drain the life out of them, feeding systems that quietly suffocate everything sacred in the human spirit.

You see a world structured not just without conscience, but for the purpose of suppressing it.

Modern civilization undermines the very qualities that nourish the soul: peace, harmony, compassion, creativity, faith.

And while you understand that every soul is manifesting the lessons necessary for its evolution, it does little to soften the shock when the profound disorientation of humanity clashes with your newfound clarity. This becomes the real challenge of the awakened one: trying to navigate a world where communities are ruled by envy and groupthink, workplaces by politics and people-pleasing, and societies by endless performance and surface morality. A world where news and media function as the central cog of a machinery that aims to sedate, gaslight, and sow ongoing division. Where surveillance is normalized, dissent is punished, and speaking truth comes with real risk. A world where science serves its funders, and objective reality is routinely denied.

When confronted with this reality, ordinary life begins to resemble a carefully crafted hallucination. What once felt familiar and trustworthy reveals itself as a landscape of psychological operations. People you once admired sound as if they're speaking through a trance, while those you once dismissed suddenly make sense. The stories you were raised on, the historical narratives that shaped your worldview, the moral binaries that formed your sense of right and wrong—all of it begins to unravel. What you mistook for truth turns out to be an elaborately constructed lie.

It's an ontological shock that tests how deeply you can remain rooted in God Consciousness while the world around you dismisses and denies it entirely. The shock of recognizing the depth of the collective darkness can exceed the shock of realizing your own true nature. Knowing *who* you are is one thing. Recognizing *what* the world has become is another. This realization is its own initiation—The Second Awakening.

You look back at your old beliefs—the narratives you defended, the judgments you cast, the illusions you accepted without question. Shame may surface when you realize how confidently you once upheld the very systems that harmed you, that were built to keep you small, anxious, and willing to hand over your power.

And now, when you try to speak truth, you find yourself misunderstood, even resented. Your clarity makes you an outcast. Your discernment is perceived as danger. Your peace comes across as indifference. It can feel like a double blow: seeing the world accelerating toward a cliff, and being punished for pointing it out. This dissonance can trigger a true crisis of faith.

To remain luminous in an upside-down world, you must be willing to see the darkness fully—not partially, not symbolically, but in its fullest expression. This gives rise to the unthinkable: that not all darkness is simply confusion—some of it is intentional. There are scrupulous forces shaping the world that are not merely unconscious but deliberate in the subjugation and exploitation of it. Some individuals do not simply forget Spirit—they are invested in preventing others from remembering. This is a harsh revelation, but an essential one: there are realms so severed from the divine that it feels impossible for light to ever return there.

This is not the stumbling lostness of ordinary humanity. It is organized, strategic, and committed to total dominance. You begin to see that the modern world isn't merely drifting into darkness—it is being steered by forces in which divine intelligence is not just absent, but inverted for purposes that are unmistakably *anti-life*.

Faith is not escaping the darkness.
Faith is carrying light into it.

But even pure evil is not a mistake. It is the threshold that pushes you from naive spirituality to embodied truth. You are being asked to look directly into the darkness—not to be consumed by it, but to outgrow the version of yourself that needed the world to be good in order to stay faithful.

And so the great return begins.

Part III

The Great Rebalancing

CHAPTER 18

THE BREAK IN THE SPELL

For most of your life, the world was presented as a stable set of meanings: what to want, what to fear, who to trust, who to dismiss, what success looks like, what failure means, what counts as "real." These meanings were so thoroughly rehearsed by everyone around you—family, schooling, media, culture—that you never thought to question them.

But there comes a moment—usually quiet, unexpected, and never at a convenient time—when you cross the threshold your inner voice has been quietly guiding you toward. A moment when the world you spent a lifetime navigating, understanding, and accommodating simply no longer fits. When the ways you shrank yourself stop working, and your impulse to stay small can no longer override your desire to be real.

This is when the foundations that once felt solid begin to flicker. The truths you inherited feel oddly hollow. The beliefs you leaned on lose their grip. You look at the same conversations, the same institutions—government, media, education, history, science, medicine—and suddenly they sound less like truth and more like a story someone else needed you to believe.

Except now—you don't.

You hear differently. You feel differently. You perceive the world not through what it claims to be but through its energy. Instead of taking people's words and actions at face value, you see *through* them. You see the fear behind their smiles. You feel the tension in their speech. You sense the emotional and physical cost of living out of alignment. You see through motives, narratives, and agendas that was once considered normal behavior. You see that nothing happens without someone wanting it to happen that way—usually to their benefit. It's so near and clear now, it leaves you puzzled why you didn't notice it before. This break in the spell is the first moment of unfiltered perception.

When the spell breaks, the framing dissolves. You see how much of what you believed was simply the consensus pressure of the people around you. You notice the mind's constant need for control, labels, and taking sides. You feel the tug-of-war between the part of you that wants to cling to the familiar and the part that refuses to go back to sleep. The world hasn't changed—but your clarity has.

With this shift comes a new orientation. You can finally acknowledge the shadows that were always there—buried beneath routine, politeness, productivity, and distraction. You see how institutions speak one language publicly and another energetically. You recognize that much of modern life—news cycles, manufactured outrage, social performance, productivity culture—is not designed to inform or unite, but to keep people fearful, preoccupied, and divided. You realize that the world, as constructed, was never meant to help you wake up. It was designed to control you.

Clarity is not cynicism—it is the end of naive innocence.

While you were aware of some of this darkness before, now seeing the mechanisms of the world doesn't make you bitter or scared—it makes you sober. And with this sobriety a new realization dawns: that the world's dysfunction only overwhelms you when you're asleep within it. That the outer world can be seen without being engulfed by the chaos. That the noise—while still deafening—doesn't have to define you. Instead, it can be used as contrast for you to feel your own signal.

And with that clarity, the external life becomes simpler to manage. What once felt threatening now looks obvious and predictable. What once felt personal now feels like other people's patterns. What was once the bane of your existence—the unknowability of life—is now your greatest ally in your journey. The world stops frightening you once you stop needing it to confirm your truth.

The break in the spell also reveals something uncomfortable: every illusion requires your participation to exist. Without your buy-in, nothing would have any power over you. Every time you silence yourself, every time you conform to avoid discomfort, every time you adopt a belief because it is socially convenient—you strengthen the very spell you are trying to wake up from. Outside powers can only operate through the implicit permission you give by abandoning yourself.

This is the hardest part of awakening: recognizing your own complicity, your own darkness. This recognition is not meant as self-blame—rather, it is to be seen as self-liberation. Because the moment you see that you helped uphold the illusion, you also realize you can withdraw your energy from it. What was maintained through unconscious agreement now dissolves through your simple awareness of it.

As your awareness deepens, a new kind of intelligence emerges. It does not shout or argue. It does not try to convince or use fear as leverage. It speaks with a simplicity that instantly dispels the shadowy complexity of mental entanglements.

This intelligence does not tell you what to think. In fact, it's not related to thought at all. It's the return of a *felt* knowing, the resonant truth so integral to divine architecture. And it is uncompromising and uncompromised. It reveals hypocrisy without the need for anger. It exposes illusion without casting blame. It guides you without demanding obedience.

This intelligence doesn't fight the world. It sees it as it is, and inspires you to take action to change it according to truth. It doesn't oppose systems—it stops mistaking them for unchangeable reality. It doesn't linger or get hung up on what something *is*—it is entirely focused on moving in the direction of what is meant to be.

You cannot explain this shift to others, nor can you force it. They hear what they hear based on their level of awareness. Someone still inside the spell will interpret your clarity as arrogance, your discernment as negativity, your independence as reckless. They are not reacting to you—they are reacting to the frequency of truth you represent. You are no longer compatible with the narratives that feed most people's illusion of safety.

When you stop participating in illusion, you become threatening to those who depend on it.

This is why awakening feels isolating at first. The conversations around you begin to sound hollow. You no longer dim to fit. You no longer tolerate the subtle violence of self-betrayal. Your clarity is too sharp for anyone to handle who hasn't awakened to it themselves. The energy with which you carry yourself—the light of your presence—exposes the smallness and inherent anxiety of the mind-identified state. People who are ready to ascend will join in your light. But many who are not will be repelled by it. And so, without announcing it, your entire life starts to reorganize itself.

You speak less but mean more. You need less but feel more abundant. You stay when it feels coherent and quietly depart when it doesn't. You don't force your presence or justify your boundaries. You no longer negotiate with the present moment. You see the beauty and purpose in everything that *is*—because everything is beautiful and purposeful by virtue of the fact that it *is*.

The break in the spell does not give you reprieve from the world. But it gives you new eyes—eyes that pick up on the intelligent design behind it all. You begin to see the playbook—the divine purpose of what happens, rather than the story the world tells you about it. You begin to see that life is not random, not cruel, not indifferent—but exquisitely oriented toward alignment.

What looked like chaos now begins to look like course-correction. What looked like punishment now feels like redirection. What you used to think of as failure you now see as refinement. What looked like loss is now a lesson in transcending attachment to form. Slowly, fear loses its authority. Not because life becomes safe, but because you no longer expect safety from the world. Instead, you look for guidance from within.

The break in the spell is the turning point, but it is only the beginning. Once you are no longer hypnotized by the collective dream of separation, you are free to participate in the deeper order underlying physical reality: the self-correcting rhythm of consciousness, the energetic nature of the universe, the meaning that is found in just being, the surrender to the intelligence that holds everything together without effort and without needing your permission.

CHAPTER 19

THE MIRROR OF LIFE

Life is not judging you—it is mirroring you. Every experience, every relationship, every difficulty is your current level of awareness reflecting itself back through form. What you get is not punishment or reward, but pure feedback showing you where even greater awareness is still possible. The mirror of life never hides anything from you. It simply offers the next thing you're ready to discover about yourself.

The mind struggles with this concept of reflection because it sees life through the lens of cause and effect. Something happens, and something follows. But life's design is not linear. When a lesson is encountered but not learned, it keeps coming back. When something remains unintegrated, it does not disappear—it reappears in different shapes until it is fully felt. The mirror repeats not to make you miserable, but to make you whole.

This is why no experience is a waste and no event is unnecessary. Whatever you avoid, deny, or refuse to feel becomes fuel for the next reflection. Lies keep circling until truth is seen. Suffering reappears where honesty is missing. Patterns reemerge until total clarity is achieved. What feels like annoying repetition is simply life pointing you back to where you're stuck so you can address it. Life is always molding you from less aware to more aware.

Everything happens for a reason—and the reason is you.

The mirror of life is so accurate, precise, and creative, it finds a way to reflect back even the slightest distortions of truth you might carry. Be it related to fear, guilt, superiority, or resentment—you will keep encountering some variation until the blockage is cleared. This is why people find themselves in the same conflicts, the same heartbreaks, the same disappointments over and over again. You can move to a new city, start a new job, change your relationship—as long as the inner entanglements stay unresolved, old patterns will repeat until denying them becomes impossible.

Once a pattern is fully seen, fully felt, fully accepted, the reflection changes from dissonance to clarity. One could even say the mirror falls away and you are now in direct contact with life—seeing it as it is, without mind chatter getting in the way. There is incredible peace and sovereignty in witnessing the harmony of all life forms interacting. In being fearless and present for the next moment. In feeling old cycles of repetition replaced by a sense of completion. This is when life stops echoing your pain because you're no longer in resistance. It supports your arrival because you're no longer trying to get somewhere.

The mirror of life only reflects what is unconscious.

The mirror does not show life—it shows you. Two people can experience the same event and see entirely different reflections. As such, you cannot escape your own frequency. You cannot pretend to be someone you're not. But the moment you stop insisting that reality should be otherwise, the reflection purifies. You begin to see without projection, without superimposing your stories. When the mirror ceases to distort, life reveals its benign design.

Life does not want your suffering. It gains nothing from your depression, your shame, your fear. No one benefits from your struggles—but everyone benefits from your awakening. The universe thrives through awareness, and every reflection is designed to awaken it in you. The more aware you become, the clearer you can hold the frequency of God Consciousness.

Whatever your life situation may be, know that you are unconditionally supported. When you suffer, the universe listens. When you resist, it waits. When you remember, it rejoices. Life's patience is infinite because its purpose is singular: to bring you back into alignment with it.

This is why even apparent setbacks are sacred. The illness that slows you down, the loss that humbles you, the failures that crush you—each is a reorientation toward alignment. When the outer world refuses to cooperate with your plans, it's not because God is being mean. It's simply because the plans you concocted were steering you away from your liberation.

Life intervenes not to punish you but to get you back on track.

Once you stop judging the reflection, you notice that life is not against you—it is *for* you in ways your mind cannot comprehend. You recognize how the smallest events start to glimmer with meaning: a chance encounter, a delay, a conversation that delivers exactly the information you needed to hear. Even as a teaching, you see the gift your students represent. Life's choreography is flawless once you are quiet enough to perceive it.

When the mirror dissolves, you recognize that every confrontation was an act of love, every ending an invitation to begin again. You stop asking for life to be different and begin asking to see it as it is. And in that seeing, suffering loses its grip and pain no longer defines you. Truth does.

CHAPTER 20

THE FEMININE RETURN

———◦———

The return of the feminine is not a trend, a movement, or a matter of reclaiming cultural space. It is the natural rebalancing of a world pulled too long in one direction. For centuries, the dominant energies of human life have been outward, forceful, analytical, and relentlessly goal-driven. These qualities built civilizations, protected life, and carved paths through wilderness—both physical and psychological.

But the structure they created was never meant to stand alone. Without the balancing presence of the feminine—receptivity, intuition, care, patience, relational warmth and depth—even strength becomes brittle. Even clarity becomes one-dimensional. Even progress becomes hollow. Life becomes all achievement and no embodiment—lost in doing, and lost to being.

But the feminine is not here to overthrow. She is here to reunite, bringing feeling to thought, meaning to productivity, intuition to logic, and connection to action.

She is not here to change who leads, but to heal how we all lead.

The feminine is not a counter-force but a harmonizing one. Where the masculine bears down and demands attention, the feminine sits back and receives affection. Where the masculine forces a response, the feminine allows stillness. Wherever the masculine clears a path, the feminine steps in to make it livable. She returns not to disrupt, but to integrate what was incomplete without her: the knowing that life does not thrive when overtaken or conquered. It thrives when honored and embraced.

Receptivity is not the absence of power. On the contrary, it is the deepest form of power because it lives in sync with life. It does not require resistance to exist. Quiet on the surface, it includes, absorbs, softens, and slowly restores everything back into divine order. She is not the force that wins the battle. She is the force that transcends the battle, making it unnecessary.

The feminine is a most profound aspect of God Consciousness.

This is why the world feels starved. There are unprecedented feats of achievement, yet a profound lack of nourishment. We have information but no wisdom to give it context, global connectivity without true intimacy, technological progress, yet no peace. The masculine mind has raced ahead, while the feminine heart has been left behind. And so her return begins—not through protest, which would betray her nature, nor through demands for sameness, which deny her uniqueness—but through embodiment, through the power of presence.

When feminine energy is allowed to return, it appears first as exhaustion with constant striving. As the quiet refusal to equate productivity with purpose. As the longing for depth in a shallow culture. As the preference for simple being over endless doing. The return of the feminine begins within the individual who realizes that life cannot be navigated by will alone—that joy cannot be forced, that meaning cannot be scheduled, that peace cannot be earned through achievement.

**The feminine is not the answer. She is
the pause that reveals the answer.**

She is the sacred interruption in a world hypnotized by overdoing. She is the whisper that calls you back to stillness when you drown in the noise of your mind. She is the intuitive current that speaks only when you become quiet enough to hear. And in that listening, a hidden truth emerges: life does not need to be managed to unfold, and love does not need to be earned to be received.

Compassion is often mistaken for softness. But true compassion is clarity. The feminine sees the wound beneath a person's defensiveness, the hurt inner child within the struggling adult, the fear that motivates aggression, the exhaustion that is the hidden cost of achievement. She does not shame what she sees. But rather, she holds space for it. And through this acceptance, she dissolves what the analytical mind can only categorize but never heal. She restores through inclusion, where the masculine attempts to correct through control.

Yet even here, she must remember her true nature. When the feminine tries to imitate the masculine—through loud demands, hierarchy, or moral superiority—she loses her center. Feminine energy withdraws when forced into battle and contracts the moment she attempts to triumph. True feminine power does not need to win. It dissolves the very need for winning.

And still, she does not judge you for forgetting her. She waits for you to become present enough for her to return. For your striving to exhaust itself. For your heart to ache for something real. For your attention to shift from surface appearance to inner truth. For you to value the unseen as much as the seen.

**The feminine flourishes wherever she
is allowed to unfold instead of being
controlled.**

The purpose of the feminine is not to rule but to realign life with God Consciousness. She exists in every human being, regardless of gender, and rises the moment one becomes willing to feel deeply, listen honestly, and inhabit the present moment fully. When she awakens, she restores what was never meant to be separated: strength and tenderness, clarity and compassion, logic and intuition, action and stillness. She does not drag the world into the past nor push it into the future—she brings consciousness back into the body, back into the now.

Her invitation is simple and yet revolutionary: turn inward. Slow down. Feel what your life is asking you to feel. Listen for the space between the words. Let your decisions arise from resonance, not project plans. Stop abandoning yourself in the name of getting somewhere. Let the heart speak before the mind interprets.

The feminine is not here to change the world. She is here to stop the world from abandoning itself.

CHAPTER 21

THE RESTORATION OF THE MASCULINE

———◇———

The restoration of the masculine is not a resurgence of dominance. It is the remembering of purpose. For generations, the masculine has been shamed, muted, distorted, or inflated—but rarely understood. What passes for strength today is ambition, confidence, and efficiency. But none of these touch the real essence. True masculine presence is rooted not in assertion, but in integrity—in the quiet strength that comes from doing the right thing. It requires no force, only the willingness to stand for what is sacred.

At its core, the masculine is not an energy of domination, but of devotion. Its instinct is to protect life's unfolding, not to control it. When healthy, it becomes the steady rhythm within which the feminine can safely expand. When wounded, it thinks it derives power from command and containment, thereby choking the very life it intends to guide. Restoration of the masculine is the dissolution of that confusion.

The masculine aligned with God Consciousness does not seek permission to exist, nor does it seek to overpower. It seeks to serve. It recognizes that restraint is a greater act of strength than force, responsibility a greater act of courage than a trophy, and listening a deeper expression of leadership than demanding attention. Without God Consciousness, the masculine becomes myopic and self-referential. But with it, the masculine is free to become open and transparent.

Modern culture has confused men about their role and conditioned women to distrust masculine structure altogether. The result is not empowerment, but chronic exhaustion across all. Compassion without boundaries leads to enabling. Direction without truth becomes tyranny. The restoration of the masculine is not a rejection of softness—it is the strength that makes space for softness to exist.

The restoration of the masculine is not about reclaiming power. It is about reclaiming self-command. A man who cannot govern his impulses cannot protect anything meaningful. A culture that idolizes indulgence will always fear the disciplined masculine, because he cannot be seduced by ease or controlled by fear. His danger is not in his aggression—it is in his incorruptibility. He cannot be bought by comfort, rattled by chaos, or manipulated by shame. He serves something higher than his own opinion.

The wounded masculine is easily identified. It is loud, reactive, and desperate to prove itself. The restored masculine, on the other hand, is quiet, anchored, and self-assured. He does not need to posture because nothing in him is up for negotiation. His value is not determined by circumstances, and his actions are not directed by collective fads. His power is not physical or intellectual—it is the unmistakable calm of a man living with God Consciousness.

The world does not need more accomplishment. It needs more presence.

This is the masculine the world longs for—not the tyrant, not the savior, but the presence that steadies the field. He feels deeply, but is not ruled by emotions. He can hold tenderness without compromising it. The masculine does not heal by rejecting strength, but by remembering the divine purpose behind it. He does not need to become "more emotional"—he just needs to become *more conscious*.

The feminine's return softens the world so the masculine can remember his true strength. The restoration of the masculine stabilizes the world so the feminine can reveal her full depth. Together, they do not act as authority over life but as the embodiment of alignment with it. Together, they form the living rhythm of God Consciousness taking form.

In every human being, this reunion follows the same pattern. The inner feminine calls you home, and the inner masculine protects you on the way and keeps you there. The feminine whispers, *Be still,* and the masculine answers, *I will guard this stillness.* The feminine says, *Feel,* and the masculine replies, *I will not run.* The feminine invites surrender, and the masculine commits, *I will see this through.*

There is nothing romantic or symbolic about this union. It is the architecture of an energetic universe. The restoration of the masculine is not the rise of man over woman, or logic over love. It is the return of order to chaos, conscience to power, and reverence to a world ruled by a runaway will.

Its leadership is quiet. Its protection is invisible. Its strength is trustworthy because it remembers its Source. The restoration of the masculine is the return of inner authority to a humanity that forgot how to stand in truth.

CHAPTER 22

YOUR INNER AUTHORITY

After realizing how life mirrors every distortion, how the feminine reclaims the field, and how the masculine restores right action, something becomes unmistakably clear: the collapse of the outer world was never the real crisis. The deeper compromise was always internal, in how easily you handed over your inner authority.

Long before anyone silenced you, you learned to silence yourself. In your desire to be part of the world, you adopted a stance of conformity. You learned that belonging required self-editing, that success meant pleasing others, that safety demanded falling in line, that love came with conditions. Ultimately, the outer world can only amplify your inner state.

Most people don't silence themselves because they have nothing to say. In fact, they prefer the distraction of noisy chatter over the discomfort of stillness. But they sense the cost of going deeper, so when they talk, it's about surface matters. They know, often without being told explicitly, which truths will destabilize the room, which doubts will threaten the tribe, which questions will cost them credibility, intimacy, employment, or peace. And so they play along. They speak in acceptable sentences. They mirror the dominant mood. They virtue signal at every turn and become fluent in the language of whatever is permitted.

Self-censorship is the belief that the consequences of authenticity outweigh those of self-betrayal.

But the soul keeps the receipts. Every time you say *yes* when you mean *no,* something deep down aches. Every time you agree when you don't, something contracts. Every time you silence your inner voice in favor of outer approval, the gap between your lived life and your integrity widens. You stay on the beaten path to avoid discomfort—but it only beats you up more.

People think burnout comes from doing too much. But actually, it comes from doing too little of what is true. The exhaustion you feel from *staying busy* is not physical—it's existential. It is the weight of being so misaligned that you're no longer at home in your own being. You've suppressed your voice for so long and so thoroughly that you only speak when it doesn't rock the boat.

Eventually, the voice goes underground. It becomes a faint whisper in the margins of your life: the discomfort you feel around people you're supposed to like, the resentment toward responsibilities you agreed to even though you felt you shouldn't, the dire sense that, with all this achieving, your life has yet to begin. But most of all, the subtle grief and panic that arise whenever life gets quiet enough for you to hear yourself.

Most people cannot tolerate silence because stillness is where their longing for truth is loudest.

Silencing yourself is not merely a personal affair—it is the result of massive cultural conditioning. Entire systems depend on incentivizing compliance, rewarding conformity, and punishing anyone who deviates from the narrative by excluding them. You are praised for being easy to work with, easy to manage, easy to understand. Being "too honest" is seen as abrasive, divisive, unstable, or arrogant. People want to surround themselves with the familiar because they want their lives to be easy.

But consciousness is not here to be easy. It is here to be real. The turning point never comes because the world finally allows you to be authentic. It comes because you've been misaligned for so long, your inner being refuses to remain silent, even if the world punishes you. When the fear of rejection can no longer cover up the ache of self-abandonment, the voice that was once a whisper begins to speak up: *I am who I am.*

That moment is rarely dramatic. It arrives as a profound fatigue—the sheer tiredness of constantly pretending. The body's wisdom begins to revolt. The nervous system refuses to fire on false directives. Pleasing others no longer feels more sacred than honoring your own peace.

This is when you recognize that the world was never the authority in the first place. The real conflict was never between you and society—it was between your inner truth and the conditioned persona you built around it.

Once this is seen, there is no stopping the light of awareness from entering every aspect of your life. It initiates a complete realignment in your words, your choices, your lifestyles. It shows up as changes that appear inexplicable from the outside. A relationship ends without a villain. A career dissolves without acrimony. A belief system is dropped without hesitation. The self is no longer interested in winning an argument. It wants to step aside and make room for more truth.

You know it's your inner authority speaking when it's quiet, steady, and free of judgment. It doesn't need to be heard or to convince anyone. It doesn't need the world to change—it simply stops participating in the illusion.

This is the beginning of an entirely different kind of life, one in which your worth is no longer measured by external validation. You no longer shrink to preserve others' comfort, and you no longer seek belonging at the cost of abandoning yourself. Your presence becomes your transmission, your boundaries arise naturally, and your integrity becomes unmistakable.

Yet even this is not the end of your evolution. Because once your true self is no longer confined, a deeper question appears: *If meaning isn't found in the world, what am I here to do? What am I here to uphold?*

The answer is not more effort, more striving, or more strategy. It is something far subtler—the inhabiting of what is real, enduring, and already complete within the human spirit. When standing in truth becomes your natural state, the questions fall away, the fears dissolve, and the outer path reveals itself on its own.

CHAPTER 23

HEALING AND EMBODIMENT

————◦————

Spirituality often begins above the neck. The mind hears a truth and reaches for healing through understanding. But understanding is only the doorway. An enlightened thought that ignores the body never leaves the mind. It can rearrange beliefs and expand perspectives, but it does not liberate the nervous system. It does not dissolve the stuck energy of memories and trauma stored in muscles, fascia, the gut, the breath, and even the whole skeletal system. A person's physical appearance speaks volumes about their inner state.

Healing is not what happens when the mind becomes wise. Healing is what happens when the body finally feels safe enough to release what the mind was hanging onto. So while you can speak the language of awakening, it has little effect when you're still vibrating with the tension of a life lived in disconnect.

The body is not merely a container for consciousness—it is the fullest expression of it. Every contraction, every instinct, every illness, every unfinished emotion is feedback to help you navigate your circumstances. Your body isn't just *there* to move you from A to B. It is your primary guidance system, receiving insights through resonance, showing you where the light of awareness has not yet penetrated. Spiritual realization is not complete until it touches your tissue, syncs with your heartbeat, flows with your breath, and integrates into your bones.

Awakening isn't complete until truth reaches the body.

The mind is prone to escape. The body can't. It is always here right now, gathering information from each new moment. It remembers every time you could not fully meet your conscience—not to punish you, but to preserve the fragments until you are capable of full integration. That's why unlearned lessons keep coming back. The body is the archive of the soul's unfinished business. What you call tension or anxiety is often emotion you never permitted yourself to feel. What you call trauma is an experience that happened faster than your level of presence could hold. The body records everything you tolerate that isn't true.

This is why spiritual bypassing brings some peace at first, but rings hollow later. You can intellectually transcend a story, but the body will keep telling it until the energetic release is felt. You can believe all you want that you have let go, but the tightening in your jaw, chest, or back will reveal otherwise. You can decide you are free, but the weight on your shoulders will speak the truth. The mind may believe something is forgiven, but the body knows whether the forgiveness is real. To embody is to consent to truth at the level of flesh.

True healing comes when you allow the body to finish what was never completed—the full arising and passing of your feelings. Whether that completion is trembling, crying, shaking, breathing, collapsing, or simply being still, the ask is to feel your aches without abandoning them. Whatever you experience, the body's only request is honesty. It's not asking you to protect it from discomfort, but to hold space while it goes through it.

This is why true awakening descends from the mind into the body. Presence is not a mental state. It is a physiological shift. It is the nervous system coming out of judgment, survival state, and victimhood, and into the openness of allowing, receiving, and flowing. It is the integrated knowing that you no longer need to brace for the next thing that could go "wrong". It is releasing the baggage of the past and coming out of resistance to life now.

Embodiment is not something you can make happen. It is the natural byproduct of the absence of resistance.

It is the end of comparing what is happening to what you think should be happening. It's the end of managing your experience and the beginning of being the container through which it flows. When the mind stops trying to direct life, the natural intelligence of your body kicks in. It tells you when to push. It tells you when to unwind. It knows how to dissolve and let go of what is not yours to carry.

Your task is not to force healing, but to remove the pressure from trying.

Whenever consciousness expands, the body is where the old version of you dissolves. You can feel a lightness and freedom of breath whenever you loosen your grip on the steering wheel. A current of softness, relaxation, and warmth takes hold when the feminine returns to the psyche. There is a settling into peace and trust, an inner knowing that right now is all that matters and the rest will sort itself out, whenever you sink into the present moment. The process may seem slow and tedious, but it is precise. It's only your mind that wants to rush through it. Your body, however, knows to take its time and waits for awareness to arrive.

When it does, the body no longer has to speak through tension, inflammation, anxiety, or fatigue. It expresses vitality, curiosity, creativity, and flow. It knows, pain is never punishment—it is the physical speaking in the language the mental cannot ignore.

With God Consciousness, you don't ask, *How do I fix myself?* You ask, *Where am I not fully alive?* Your anxiety doesn't need a story. Your emotions don't need constant analysis. Not every sensation needs a reason. The body doesn't care about *why* and *who caused it.* It doesn't care if it happened yesterday or in a past lifetime. To experience true well-being, you must be willing to feel your feelings fully, right now, without abandoning them.

You cannot awaken without your body. In fact, you awaken *in* your body. Any disconnect only serves to delay. The deeper the realization, the quieter the body becomes. This is where wellness arises from. A healthy body is not a perfect body. It is a body that has nothing left to suppress.

CHAPTER 24

THE MEANINGFUL LIFE

When God Consciousness is absent, life feels random, empty, and disconnected. We convince ourselves that sacrifices today will buy freedom tomorrow. That stimulation equals aliveness. That being busy equals being successful. That more options means more purpose. Yet with so much meaning all around us, why do so many still feel empty?

When we start living inside a mind-made story that has ideas but no direction, options but no orientation, we drift. It's not for lack of interesting things to do in this world. But because we've lost the inner stillness needed to *feel* the meaning already built into life.

The modern age suffocated divine meaning when each person became the narrator of their own mini-universe. Every opinion was declared a truth. Every photo became part of a personal brand. Instead of living from mystery, entire generations were trained to strategize, optimize, and execute—and told they were the problem when the plan didn't pan out. Genuine alignment was replaced by ambition, identity, productivity, ideology, and performance. But life's meaning cannot be manufactured or personalized. It can only be *participated in*. It reveals itself the moment we stop trying to control what is meant to be witnessed.

Meaning disappears the moment we try to manufacture it.

Every incoherent reality—personal or collective—must eventually collapse back into divine order and preserve whatever is true. The universe expands into the unsustainable only to reveal what cannot endure. It lets illusion run its course until illusion exhausts itself.

This is why the collapse of artificial meaning feels so painful: we were taught that fulfillment was something we had to invent. We chased it like a dog chasing its own tail—never catching the very thing that only appears when we stop reaching for it. We searched for significance in form instead of in the intelligence animating the form. We asked life to save us, validate us, reward us—never realizing that the longing itself was the sign we had forgotten our place inside something infinitely larger than identity.

The good news is that meaning never disappears. It cannot. It is inherent to the design of existence. What disappears is only our capacity to *feel* it. But it returns the moment we stop manipulating life and begin relating to it as something to align with and serve. When the inner life and outer life stop competing, meaning becomes immediate—natural, effortless, and as unmistakable as breath.

**Meaning returns not when we decide
what matters, but when we stop
resisting what already does.**

The real source of meaning has nothing to do with belief, achievement, or legacy. It is the participation in the co-creative process. It might be a paradox to the mind, but the more aligned we become with reality as it is—not as we wish to shape it—the more meaningful everything becomes, including the ordinary, the temporary, and the imperfect. Meaning does not depend on outcome. It is not a mental construct. It is the felt sense of being inside a coherent universe.

This is why a meaningful life will not come from a new philosophy, a new myth, a new leader, or a new world order. It will come when we stop chasing it on the outside and rediscover our connection to Source on the inside. Anything we do from that place is meaningful. Any action we take from there has integrity. Living with God

Consciousness is stepping back into the rhythm of what is meant to be. The tree does not need a reason to grow. The ocean is not on a mission. The child does not need to justify its laughter. Meaning is not found, but inherited, not from the mind, but from beyond it.

Collective meaning returns the same way individual meaning does. When society stops crowning itself as the source of creation, something ancient begins to sweep again through the human energy field. What once felt like emptiness turns into spaciousness. What once felt like chaos is now seen as the pattern that takes us back to order. What once felt like unjust suffering reveals itself to be an invitation to return to truth.

Divine intelligence is only hidden when we're too distracted to see it.

When the world begins to realign, the qualities of a meaningful life become unmistakable: a quiet trust, a natural steadiness, a sense of belonging, an effortless clarity, a gratitude that arises on its own, and a deeper participation in the moment. Life no longer feels like something we drag behind us or push ahead of us. It begins to feel like something we move *with*. The sense of separation—from yourself, from others, from God Consciousness—fades as resistance dissolves.

Meaning returns when we stop placing personal significance above the intelligence that holds all things together. In surrender, order reveals itself and everything finds its place. This intelligence is not a theory to grasp. It is felt through the embodied practices of presence, honesty, integrity, reverence, and the quiet desire to be of service. When you align with what resonates, the world is no longer a puzzle to decode—it becomes a field you naturally belong to.

A meaningful life is not a single realization but an ongoing willingness to inhabit reality as it is, rather than filtering it through the self-concerned mind. It is living in such a way that nothing in you is pretending and you only act from the place within you that cannot be manipulated or co-opted. Meaning has never been absent. What returns is our capacity to participate in it.

CHAPTER 25

SACRED LEADERSHIP

⸻◦⸺

Leadership, in its sacred form, does not gather attention, seek admiration, or pull energy toward the individual who carries it. The true leader disappears behind the work. What becomes visible is not personality, charisma, or self-importance, but the order and devotion with which they tend to what has been entrusted to them. When you lead with God Consciousness, you do not stand in front—you stand *for*. You hold the weight that others cannot yet hold. Leadership is not a preference or a privilege. It is a summons that arrives only when your connection has been restored.

In the modern age, leadership has been confused with visibility. Titles, platforms, influence, and amplification have replaced the older understanding of leadership as inner capacity, moral clarity, and spiritual steadiness. Even if imperfect in practice, that compass once existed. Somewhere along the way, we came to believe that the leader is the one who shines brightest, speaks loudest, or occupies the highest platform.

From a spiritual perspective, the opposite is true. The more awakened a being becomes, the less they need to generate brightness—because light radiates naturally from a life aligned with truth. The more deeply they are rooted in God Consciousness, the less they need to be seen. Their presence carries its own authority. Their integrity is the illumination. Their service is the signal. Their leadership is the byproduct, not the performance.

It is only the insecure leader who needs the world to know who is leading.

Sacred leadership is the art of carrying power without being possessed by it. Its root motivation is never ambition, but necessity—the inner knowing that something must be upheld in order for life to remain in truth. While the mind asks, *How far can I go?* conscience asks, *What must be protected?* A true leader never says, "Follow me." A true leader says, "Let's do the right thing, regardless of political consequence."

Mind-based leadership builds identity by competing for roles and recognition. Sacred leadership dissolves identity through service. The ego wants the position and clings to it, always seeking more. The soul accepts responsibility without attachment, stepping forward only as long as the calling is present. A leader who lives in their head becomes the center of their story. A leader guided by Spirit becomes an instrument. There is no glory in being the instrument—only loyalty to the work of truth.

That work is always the same: to call forth the divine order behind the form—rightness, clarity, alignment, harmony. The immature leader leads people. The mature leader tends to the unfolding of God Consciousness. Their loyalty is not to special interests, lobbyists, or the groupthink of the moment. It is not to the survival of a party or the applause of the crowd. It is to the principle that governs the field. If their own side is wrong, they will stand alone. If truth requires rebuilding, they will not preserve a failing structure. If integrity requires silence, they will not speak to gain praise.

Sacred leadership does not protect its position. It protects what is sacred.

Holding clarity in the midst of distortion is one of the great tests. It is the core initiation of higher consciousness. Most people want the feeling of guidance without the friction of actually doing the work. They want the coziness of inclusion without the discipline required for alignment. The sacred leader cannot participate in this. They do not bend truth to preserve relationships. They do not offer comfort when transformation is required. They embody clarity and steadiness to such a degree that their presence cuts through distortion like a blade through fog.

The defining mark of sacred leadership is the absence of self-centered ambition—not the suppression of it, but the transcendence of it. A leader may still carry a strong self-image, but the self-image is no longer steering. They may still experience fear, but fear no longer decides. They may still feel desire, but desire no longer hijacks the mission. Real leadership—whether in a family or a nation—is not the absence of ego. It is ego held in its rightful place by something far larger.

A life lived in service to God Consciousness always puts the self second.

Divine order is not imposed order or authoritarian control. It is the natural order that emerges when truth isn't manipulated. Anyone connected to God Consciousness can feel the instant something is off. This is why a conscious citizenry is feared: no propaganda can hide the intention behind a twisted truth.

Sacred leadership is never about shaping a world that flatters the leader. It is about aligning the world with what needs to be done. A leader who serves their own vision creates followers. A leader who serves order creates leaders.

This is the quiet paradox of sacred leadership: the more authentic the leader, the less attention they require. Their worth is not measured by how many people obey them, but by how many people can stand without them. The smaller the leader's need to be central, the more stable and enduring everything becomes around them. They lead not from above, but from the field within.

> **Leadership begins not when you are**
> **ready to be seen, but when you are ready**
> **to not matter.**

And so the question shifts. Not *Who will follow me?* but *What am I willing to carry when no one is watching?* Not *How do I gain influence?* but *Can I stay aligned when it costs me status, comfort, certainty, or approval?* Not *How do I change the world?* but *Can I remain faithful to truth even when the world refuses to change?*

This is the turning point the world is entering now: leadership is no longer a career choice. It is an energetic responsibility. Wherever there is confusion, someone must hold clarity. Wherever there is fragmentation, someone must stand in integrity. Wherever truth begins to flicker, someone must guard the flame—even if no one ever knows who kept it alive.

CHAPTER 26

THE NEW SCIENCE

For centuries, science and spirituality stood on opposite sides, each convinced the other had misunderstood reality. Science trusted what could be known and measured. Spirituality trusted the unknown and the intangible. One built its worldview from objects and the laws of physics. The other built its wisdom from experience and inner revelation. They did not disagree because one was right and the other wrong. They disagreed because they were studying different layers of the same truth.

Classical science assumed that reality was solid, predictable, and externally irrevocable, no matter who was observing it. The universe was a machine, life was a coincidence, consciousness was a side effect of the brain, and truth was whatever could be repeated under controlled conditions. That worldview gave us technology, medicine, massive industries, and a sense of mastery over nature.

But it also produced an existence stripped of mystery. A world where education robs you of curiosity. A disconnected society held together—less by cultural integrity, more by similar consumption patterns. A world limited to surface reality, where what can't be explained is dismissed, what can't be proven is ignored, and what can't be controlled is denied.

Yet recently, a quiet shift has begun at the edges of physics, biology, and cognitive science—compelled by the apparent limitations of the old world view. The deeper science looks, the less solid the world becomes. Physical objects dissolve into vibrating molecules. Energy dissolves hard facts into probabilities. Matter shows itself to respond to who's watching. The observer can no longer stand outside the experiment with the mind a passive witness. Consciousness, once dismissed as a byproduct, has begun to reappear—not as philosophy, but as a variable. This variable is well on the way to becoming the underlying principle of a completely new arena where the universe is no longer a machine, but a field that reacts, adapts, responds, and—to the surprise of many scientists—participates.

Quantum physics is not out to "prove spirituality." It is simply in the process of removing the illusion that matter is the final authority. Suddenly, the smallest building blocks of existence no longer behave like objects—they behave like potential partners in a co-creative process. They do not sit still waiting to be studied—they shift depending on how they are observed. As such, in the space where the formless becomes form, and the unknown becomes known—at the junction where the human notion of *reality* begins—the universe is not a thing, it's a conversation.

Reality is not defined, nor discovered—it is participated in.

This is not a mystical claim. It is a scientific one. The more precise the instruments become, the more they reveal that the foundation of life is not certainty but possibility. It doesn't consist of solids, but of vibration. Instead of separation, there is entanglement. What spirituality calls *oneness*, science is beginning to call *nonlocality* in *the unified field*. What spirituality calls *intention-setting* and *the law of attraction*, science thinks of as *the observer effect*. What spirituality calls *Source*, science is beginning to suspect may be consciousness itself.

The shift is not that science is becoming spiritual. The shift is that science—like the humans who occupy the space—is shedding an older version of itself and becoming more humble in the process. The old confidence that equations would eventually explain everything has softened into curiosity. The universe is no longer treated as a machine to be understood, but as a mystery to be explored. Laws remain, but they are less mechanical and more relational in nature.

The mind that once demanded proof is now willing to ask different kinds of questions. It's no longer "What is the world made of?" but "Why does it respond the way it does?" No longer "How does consciousness emerge from matter?" but "How does matter emerge *within* consciousness?" No longer "What is real?" but "What is real *when observed?*" This represents a big leap for the scientific community.

Science evolves the moment it stops interrogating reality and begins listening to it.

It is important to emphasize that spirituality is not being validated—it is being rediscovered through another doorway. Ancient teachings did not need particle accelerators to know that intention shapes experience, that perception is creative, that outer reality reflects your inner state. They simply studied life from the inside out. Modern science, after centuries of dissecting nature, has reached the same insight from the opposite direction: truth is not found by breaking the universe apart, but by realizing that nothing within it is separate.

Science provided a structured approach to proceed with the mind in a material world and in economically sustainable contexts. It is now at the seam where external and internal meet. Eventually, it will reach the point where it discovers that inner and outer dissolve. Both science and spirituality are bound to arrive at the same conclusions, just through a different lens.

**Whatever path you take, life is designed
to take you home.**

This is where the old scientific worldview ends and the new one begins—not in certainty, but in the wonder of self-realization. A reality that is participatory. Where perception is not passive. Where thoughts are not private. Where attention is not neutral. Where truth is not discovered, but aligned with.

As this becomes clear, the old culture of answers gives way to a new culture of questions—ones that reach far beyond technique and touch existence itself: *What worldview emerges when consciousness is not a random byproduct of matter, but the intentional medium of reality? What happens when every observer realizes that seeing gives shape, and presence influences outcomes? What to make of personal responsibility when the building blocks of reality are not separate, but entangled and interactive?* These are no longer academic curiosities. They are spiritual thresholds. The moment the observer is included in the equation, every life becomes an experiment in truth.

We are exiting the age of separation—where humans looked *at* reality—and entering the age of participation, where we are *part of* reality. You are not a spectator standing outside the universe. You are a participant in its unfolding. Every act of attention is an act of creation. Every moment of awareness a subtle calibration of the field. The universe doesn't need to be decoded. It needs you to be present.

CHAPTER 27

SURRENDER AND PARTICIPATION

⸻◆⸻

The world has taught us to move through life by plans, by focus, by managing outcomes, by force—by using willpower as the primary instrument of creation. But what we call *control* is often just fear and avoidance manifesting as strategy. The mind does not trust reality to unfold without its supervision. It thinks *alignment* means conforming your circumstances to your expectations. It creates to-do lists where perspective and space are needed. It feels urgency, unaware that divine timing is already exact. It treats life as if it were asleep at its own wheel.

But the more one awakens, the clearer it becomes that life is not asking you to take over. It is asking you to move with its rhythm—to stop interfering with the intelligence already present in every seed, every heartbeat, every sunrise. Every trigger points to something that needs healing. Every unexpected event is an invitation to expect less and flow more.

**We're not being asked to fix the
world—only to stop breaking it.**

The mind thinks surrender is passive, when it's
the most intimate form of participation. It is
the recognition that life is not happening *to* you,
but *because* of you, and ultimately *for* you. It is the
end of trying to chase goals and force outcomes and
the beginning of living in a reality full of higher
intelligence, creativity, and wonder. Surrender does not
say, "Do nothing." It says, "Do only what is true." It
does not hold you back. It clarifies the path forward,
providing the fuel for complete dedication and focus.

In true surrender, doing no longer feels like pushing.
It's more akin to listening. Action arises in response
to what is happening—not in reaction to what was
planned, predicted, or calculated. In this natural
responsiveness, there is no space for interior debate or
external argument. In alignment with Spirit, there is no
need to make life yield to your story.

**What needs to be done becomes
obvious when the doer is no longer
trying to be someone.**

This is the essence of co-creation: not two distinct powers collaborating, but one intelligence passing through two perspectives. The drop does not see itself as separate from the ocean. It moves with the greater current, sometimes as a majestic wave, sometimes as a little ripple. But never without the distinct purpose of whatever shape it's taking right now. In the same way, participation in the unfolding life becomes effortless when the individual no longer assumes they are the origin of anything.

Surrender does not erase effort. In fact, it makes you busier than ever. Source waits patiently for you to reconnect and come online. Once you do, the real show begins. Without the friction created by urgency, self-concern, and imagined control, the floodgates to creation open wide, and action becomes clean, precise, and incredibly prolific. You do what wants to be real, feel when you're asked to feel, move when compelled to move, and speak when spoken through. Your life becomes a continuous stream of small moments of truth-telling and micro-acts of alignment. And while big events might arise from this, the real sign of connectedness is that there's no longer a split between "my life" and life itself.

The world does not suffer from a lack of action. It suffers from a lack of aligned action.

Every problem humanity faces stems from a single illusion: that life is not already self-correcting. The truth of this becomes unmistakable when you're connected. You experience yourself not as separate from the field you contribute to. But rather, as one cell in the body of the whole. When you act from truth, your creativity opens, your trust deepens, even your immune system responds. Contrast that with acting from fear, where your body tightens, your anxiety spikes, and your vision narrows. Surrender is nothing mystical—it's the moment you refuse to endure the suffering of swimming against the current and finally trust that life knows what it's doing.

The deepest form of surrender is not to a remote higher power. It's to living in sync with the accuracy of the moment. To the inner knowing that arises when you stop demanding external answers and allow things to be. To the silence that precedes insight. To the timing that reveals itself only when you stop rushing and step back far enough to see the whole picture.

And then, almost without effort, the world that once felt heavy begins to feel orchestrated—not predetermined, not controlled by an external hand, but like a dance that continuously surprises both dancers. An aliveness that only knows where it's going as the direction takes shape. A shared expression between the Creator and the created.

**Devotion is not obedience. It is the
recognition of shared authorship.**

You enter the co-creative state when you no longer need to defend yourself against life. When you stop evaluating each situation for advantage or risk. When you stop looking for meaning in each moment and simply inhabit it. Once you do this, even the most ordinary events become alive again, and simplicity becomes sufficient—if not blissful. Doing is no longer a tactic for control, but a series of gestures of alignment. Each word you speak is from the center instead of the surface. You move from accepting your fate to participating in it.

This is the quiet end of spiritual seeking. It happens—not because you've understood everything—but because you no longer need to. You've recognized that surrender does not give you power—it removes the illusion that you ever needed it. It returns you to the only place that's real and where you're meant to stand: inside the flow of what is already happening.

You are not here to get life right. You are here to let life move through you without obstruction. The work is not to act more. The work is to interfere less. And so the final question is not *What should I do?* but *What am I still resisting?* Because once resistance dissolves, participation is automatic.

CHAPTER 28

THE CONSERVATIVE PRINCIPLE

⎯⎯◆⎯⎯

Once you stop silencing your inner voice, a quiet but revolutionary shift occurs: the instinct to gravitate towards what is real. Not the preservation of tradition for the sake of nostalgia, not the defense of ideology to reinforce belonging and identity, not the clinging to old forms out of fear—but a more profound, spiritual conservatism born of clarity. When the noise of the mind-identified state falls away, it becomes obvious that much of what the world calls *progress* is simply activity without direction, innovation without depth, and novelty without meaning. When your consciousness awakens, it frees you from that cultural slumber, and you no longer need to constantly seek the new. You seek the true.

This is the real conservative instinct—the natural impulse to protect what is aligned with life, truth, and universal law, and to let everything else go without sentimentality. God Consciousness doesn't create systems, it builds on principles. It doesn't rely on institutions, but inspires you to rely on your own inherent integrity. It doesn't resist change, only the inversion of meaning. When you no longer react from the mind, but respond to circumstances from the heart, you recognize that a civilization crumbles when it forgets what it stands on, even as it celebrates its evolution.

For most of human history, conservatism meant guarding what the past had discovered. Now it means protecting what consciousness already knows. The deeper the awakening, the clearer it becomes that truth is not progressive. Truth does not require updating, branding, or endless revisions. It doesn't need research committees, collective bargaining, or legal precedent. Truth does not need justification. It is always ancient, always current, always self-validating. The only thing that evolves is the mind's relationship to it.

**Awakening is the instinct to preserve
what is real.**

And so the individual, once untethered from the collective narrative, senses their task is no longer to follow the patterns of the world—but to discover what the world has forgotten. In this way, the conservative principle is not resistance to the future—it is a refusal to abandon the eternal for what is fashionable and fading. Because that which is essential is not loud, does not trend, doesn't require cultural approval, and never ceases to be relevant.

Real truth is simple, coherent, and now. It does not need an audience—only a witness. Once seen, it marks the end of spiritual consumerism. The awakened person no longer chases practices, protocols, or ecstasy in hopes of becoming more advanced. God Consciousness is not a state to be figured out. It comes when you release what is unnecessary—which is most things the mind ascribes value to. Your only task is to become vigilant with what you give your attention to. To conserve the energy you don't feel called to use. To stay silent when there's no reason to speak.

To be conservative is to be intentional, discerning, present, and real.

And this is where the inner and outer worlds collide. Because the individual who has reclaimed inner authority and refuses self-silencing is now confronted with the reality that most modern structures are built on opposite values: surface issues matter more than depth, individual negotiation more than universal truth, image and appearance more than core essence, economic growth more than well-being indicators. To live aligned with the conservative principle is to accept a quiet exile—not from society itself, but from its hypnosis.

Yet the paradox is this: the one who steps out of the collective trance becomes more capable of serving life than the one who remains committed to it. They are no longer operating from compulsion, imitation, or fear. They are no longer trying to fix the world by force, activism, or outrage. They are preserving something far more vital: the conditions in which God Consciousness can remain awake. That preservation never happens through ideology—only through honest embodiment.

And then it becomes clear why the crisis of faith and pursuit of false freedoms was necessary. Every distortion points back to clarity. Every lie gives rise to truth. The deepest darkness enables ascension to the highest light. The conservative principle is not a political position or a return to the past. It's the place from which you live once you realize that nothing essential can be taken from you.

No one in the world needs to be saved. But something in the human spirit must be protected: its capacity to perceive truth without distortion, to live without self-betrayal, to honor what is eternal even when the world tries hard to discard it. That is the real work ahead.

CHAPTER 29

THE RENEWED EARTH

The renewed earth is not a new creation. It does not need to be envisioned, engineered, or imagined. It requires no blueprints, projections, or elaborate governance. It certainly does not require the type of organization the mind believes is necessary.

The renewed earth rests on an order that has always been here—obscured only by the mind's attempt to control what it cannot comprehend. It is not a utopian fantasy, nor the invention of idealists. It is the natural consequence of God Consciousness reclaiming its place as the organizing principle of human life.

For most of history, humanity has built outward. Structures, systems, empires were erected with the belief that progress meant adding layers of complexity. But complexity without consciousness eventually collapses under its own weight. In truth, complexity is not the sign of an advanced civilization but of a disconnected one. Life, at its core, is simple.

What we are witnessing now is not the failure of governments or institutions. It is the exhaustion of unconscious creation. Any civilization built on separateness will fracture. Any culture built on competition will drain its own vitality. And when personal identity takes precedence over universal truth, reality itself stops cooperating.

The earth is renewed the moment we stop resisting reality.

People who inhabit God Consciousness live differently, think differently, breathe differently. They educate their children differently. They engage with medicine, nature, community, and governance differently. They draw their values—not from social consensus—but from a multidimensional awareness the mind cannot reach.

God Consciousness does not *construct* the future. It reveals the future that becomes possible once the distortion of mind-identification dissolves. Just as a puddle reflects the sky only when its ripples settle, only a clear conscience can reflect divine order. The collapse of the old world is simply the clearing of noise so meaning can be perceived again.

The renewed earth does not arrive through force, ideology, or regime change. True change emerges when a collective shifts from living a mind-led life to a Source-led one. When inner alignment shapes external action. When enough individuals stop seeing themselves as separate little humans trying to "win" at life. When the world no longer organizes itself around fear, lack, or the need for control.

In such a world, systems soften. Hierarchies dissolve. People bond over shared humanity rather than extracting value from one another. Intelligence becomes distributed instead of owned. Wisdom becomes shared instead of suppressed. Abundance replaces competition as the default orientation. Power flows through presence rather than dominance. Healing becomes the natural state, not the rare exception.

The old world rewarded those who climbed over others. The renewed earth recognizes only those who stand in truth.

In the old paradigm, the world was treated as a resource to be mined. In the renewed one, life becomes a relationship—economic, ecological, social, and spiritual systems reorganize themselves around reciprocity rather than transaction. Value stops being tied to scarcity and begins arising from contribution, service, and shared uplift. Leadership ceases to be a circus of elites, media stops functioning as propaganda, and knowledge is no longer weaponized. The renewed earth is not *better*—it is *truer*. It reflects a humanity living from its connection with Source, rooted in the interdependence that was always the real foundation of existence.

The renewed earth is not the result of superior innovation. It does not emerge from breakthroughs in equations or physics. It has nothing to do with colonizing new planets. It arises from remembering that intelligence is already woven through everything alive. When human beings stop acting as the designers of the world and begin acting as participants within it, the question shifts from *How do we control reality?* to *How do we cooperate with it?*

In the renewed earth, belonging is no longer negotiated through identification with one group or another. It arises naturally from one's relationship with the higher power that animates all life. Communities with shared interests or cultural heritage still exist, but only as vessels for honoring divine expression—not as bunkers that separate one soul from another. Sameness suffocates God's creativity. Diversity protects the human species.

Self-worth is no longer earned through people-pleasing or climbing ladders. Relationships are no longer defined by utility or extraction. Love is no longer conditional or circumstantial. There is a deep recognition that how you treat others is a reflection of how you treat yourself. The spiritual and material no longer sit on separate shelves, because seen clearly, they point to the same place.

The renewed earth is not a fantasy. It is simply what emerges when awareness matures. A species that no longer fears its own thoughts stops building systems that punish itself. A mind that no longer exploits the body stops exploiting nature. A person who is connected treats the world as one. The renewed world is what remains when the illusion of separation has exhausted itself.

And the illusion *is* running its course. You can feel it in the growing refusal to live from the nervous system of survival. You can sense it in the collective fatigue with division. You can hear it in the rising hunger for sincerity, presence, depth, and grounded truth. What comes next is not a new philosophy, but a return to life lived without the need to defend yourself against it.

Most importantly, the renewed earth does not require everyone to awaken. It requires only enough awake beings to carry their light into the spaces they inhabit. A civilization can shift through the small but steady acts of alignment performed by very few.

Bringing God Consciousness into daily life is not a revolution—yet it carries the power of one. The kindness you extend to a stranger in a supermarket line ripples instantly. The humility with which you lead your team elevates everyone involved. The honesty you bring into your relationships awakens the same honesty in others, and every person touched becomes a torchbearer in their own right.

Living in truth awakens the truth in others.

God Consciousness is a field—a frequency carried by those who live without inner conflict, without spiritual performance, without the constant bargaining of a self-centered mind. The renewed earth arises from within this frequency. It emerges through those who no longer resist the intelligence already moving through all things.

And so the question is no longer *What world do we create?* but *What world are we willing to inhabit?* No longer *What can we achieve?* but *What are we willing to embody?* The renewed earth will not descend from the sky or save humanity from itself. It will not come through prophecy, technology, or movements promising a new hope. It will crystallize through those who stop living in contradiction with what they know to be true.

The foundation of the next world is laid in consciousness. It begins every time someone refuses to abandon awareness for fear. Every time someone chooses inner alignment over outer image. Every time truth is honored more than conformity. Every time presence replaces pretending. Which means the future is not something you wait for, or watch being built. It is something you can start participating in right now.

The world ahead is not waiting for better systems, better policies, or better inventions. It is waiting for truer beings.

CHAPTER 30

THE DESIGN OF LIFE

Every plan falls apart the moment it meets reality—not because life is chaotic, but because creation is infinite, precise, and *real-time*. When countless forces converge into the energy of *now*, the mind cannot keep up. It can't even predict tomorrow.

Even the distinction between "good" and "bad" loses meaning over time. Blessings turn into teachers. Setbacks turn into catalysts. Life moves in arcs too vast for the mind to comprehend. All we can ever do is show up and respond to what is already there.

When form breaks, it is not evidence of God's absence. It is evidence of truth finally asserting itself. Much of what we call accidents, failures, or tragedies is really life releasing what no longer serves our evolution. A relationship ending, a business dissolving, an illness slowing us down—these are not interruptions to the plan. They *are* the plan.

Of course it hurts when our attachments are severed. The mind panics, the heart grieves, and the ego resists the loss of meaning it once clung to. We tremble when asked to let go of certainty, roles, identities—even the illusion of permanence. But all of it points to one place: the quiet dismantling of the mind and the emergence of God Consciousness.

For generations, we mistook activity for vitality. We believed more choices meant more clarity, that technical innovation signaled human progress, that chasing outcomes could secure for tomorrow what we felt was missing today. In the process, we sacrificed the entire space in between. We built a world where purpose was tied to achievement and every longing was met with the material. And when anxiety, loneliness, and despair tried to alert us to the misalignment, we built even more systems to numb ourselves to it.

All of this arose from the mind-identified state—the belief that life's design is ours to invent, when in truth it is ours to recognize. Nothing needs to be figured out. Nothing needs to be forced. Creation is not a script. It is a live unfolding. Just as an artist cannot know the final painting until the last stroke lands, the universe does not know what the formless looks like until it takes shape.

Not knowing is not a threat. It is the thrill of co-creation.

Life is self-correcting. Everything false grows heavy. Everything dark moves toward light. Everything that is stuck eventually forces itself to the surface. Everything out of tune grows louder until it is addressed. All things point back to truth. The only real question is whether we cooperate with this return or continue resisting it.

Divine order is not fragile. It is relentless. When a person refuses to evolve from within, life evolves them from without. When nostalgia keeps us clinging to the obsolete, we feel ourselves held back. When we keep a situation alive out of fear, life ends it for us through pressure and breakdown. It can feel harsh, but beneath it all is a choreography that will not let us remain misaligned without asking us to feel the price. Pain is not cruelty in this design. It is feedback—life saying, *This is the cost of living in separation from God Consciousness.*

We are living through the end of a long forgetting. There will be other cycles, but this one is immense. Life cannot sustain itself on exploitation. Conscience cannot speak when we drown in thought. Truth cannot rise when everything becomes a negotiation. We've built a world on the premise that separation is real—and have suffered convincingly inside the institutions born of that illusion.

We've wandered to the edges of ourselves, mistaking choice for freedom and collecting achievements that evaporate as quickly as morning mist. The signal of God Consciousness has grown faint beneath the noise.

**We've abandoned natural law and
wonder why life feels so far from itself.**

Our forgetting, however, is not to condemn ourselves. It's a curriculum we've chosen at the grandest scale. Life has been shaping us—not through punishment, but by letting the consequences of our choices ripen until we ripen with them. The collapse we are witnessing is not doom—it is simply the end of what is not true. And there is much that is not true. Those in power who cannot carry truth fear it, and so they censor it—because on some level they recognize that truth would set everyone free.

Returning to truth is not a return to the past. It is not a retreat into innocence or a reversal into earlier stages of awareness. It is a return to what is real, but with far greater awareness than before.

In this sense, the return to the design of life is the greatest leap forward. We inverted ourselves to test the limits, and now we return with clarity, humility, and the wisdom of having been mistaken—and corrected—by a love we never had to earn and which was never going to give up on us.

Peace returns when a civilization turns to presence, authenticity, meaning, and stillness.

The choreography of return is visible everywhere—in the refusal to live by scripts written by exploitative interests. In the irreverence toward institutions that once dictated norms. In workplace cultures shaking loose old expectations. In the revisiting of history and the unraveling of the narratives we were told about it. In the rising suspicion of headlines and the question, *Who paid for this story?* You can feel it in the steady courage of those who will no longer speak against what they know, even when truth costs them status or security.

This is not the noise of new confusion. It is the rumble of clarity emerging. It is reality separating itself from our mental attachment to falsehoods. It's the preparation of the soil for tenderness to grow, when you finally see how hard it is to be here and still choose truth.

In the design of life, nothing essential is ever lost. What matters is carried through the dark by the very darkness that appears to threaten it. Every shadow points to the light that will dissolve it once the object of distortion falls away.

The invitation, then, is not to predict the future but to participate in it when it arrives as the *now*—to move in ways that create no resistance in the field, to act in ways that do not divide your inner and outer life, to become a quiet force of alignment that others recognize.

You know you are aligned when the simplest thing becomes sufficient—when one honest act feels larger than the most elaborate performance. When being part of the happening matters more than controlling the outcome. When honoring what is real outweighs every lure of distraction. When the present moment feels fuller than the one you're preparing for.

Nothing needs to be overthrown. The universe always reorganizes around truth. The collapse of what is false is the birth of what is real. What looks like disorder is simply life reasserting its design. Divine law cannot be broken—only delayed.

The world is not ending. It is remembering.

EPILOGUE

———◆———

Every journey ends in stillness, not because nothing remains, but because what remains can no longer be spoken. The mind can walk beside you for a long time, maybe even all the way to this page, but it cannot cross the threshold. Language dissolves where truth becomes felt rather than understood. The words you have read were never destinations. They were temporary footprints—disappearing the moment you look directly at what is now unmistakably clear.

There is a small pause between every inhale and exhale when the body is still, where it has not yet been revealed which direction the breath will move next. That pause is where God lives. Not above, not beyond—but quietly inside the rhythm of arrival and release. If you expect you distort the arrival. If you react you prevent the release. But if you allow every moment to be—you flow.

This is what is meant by not getting in the way of the intelligence that moves through galaxies and grains of dust, through vast cycles of expansion and return. This intelligence is always there. You only don't experience it when you're too distracted from its nearness.

All the seeking that brought you here—the questions, the analyzing, the dark nights, the quiet revelations—was just the mind circling the place where it finally stops insisting on its version of reality. Now the circle closes. And what remains is what was here before the striving: this breath, this clarity, this simple moment that demands nothing and gives everything.

As you fall in line with divine rhythm—as you infuse intention with surrender—you no longer see life happening—you experience what silently animates it. And each time you rest here—before reaching for the next conclusion, before rehearsing who you think you need to be—life remembers itself through you.

The earth breathes through trees. The oceans breathe through tides. Time breathes through seasons. And God breathes through you. A quiet truth spoken at the right moment, the smallest gesture of honesty, a short prayer before a meal, the blink-of-a-moment choice to not betray yourself—these are all forms of alignment. They restore truth to a world still recovering from generations who spent holding its breath.

And so the ask now is not to search more, but to stay here. You do not need to know what comes next. You only need to stay available to what is already on its way.

You are not leaving this book wiser. You are leaving it more at peace.

Life continues. The tremors of a world built on misalignment will settle the moment you return to truth.

And God—ever the conservative—will guide you home.